Excerpts from The Prophetic Biography

Ibn Kathir

Translated & Comments by Al Reshah

Alreshah.net

Canada

Alreshah
www.Alreshah.net

Publisher's Note: This is a translation of book without change of meaning as best as the translator could achieve with few comments in the footnote to clarify.
 If any error is found, please contact us through our website alreshah.net.

Book Layout © 2017 BookDesignTemplates.com

Excerpts from The Prophetic Biography/ Ibn Kathir. -- 1st ed.
ISBN 9781775394266

Contents

The author's foreword

In the name of Allah, the Merciful, it is You we ask for help:

Many and kind thanks are to God and peace be upon His elite servants. I bear witness that there is no god but Allah alone, that has no partner. It is a virtuous witness, clear of polytheism, witness of who seeks refuge with Allah from Satan and fancy and adheres to Qur'an revealed to the Messenger of God, the best of His servants, peace be upon him, and may God be pleased with him, his companions, wives, descendants and followers.

Then after, science and knowledge require us not to neglect the remarkable dates in Islam and these related to the Prophet. They include much information and important benefits, which no scholar can do without. I would like to leave a note in this regard to be an introduction. It is about tracing the ancestry of the Prophet, his biography and his prophecy foretokens, as well as tracing post-Muhammed Islam.

Tracing ancestry of Muhammed, peace be upon him

He is of Adam's decedents. He is "Abu Alqasem"[1] Muhammed and Ahmed[2], through whom blasphemy is eliminated,

---

[1] the system of naming used in Arab Culture where the elder Son / Daughter is used it laterality translates to " Father of " and Al Qasem is first born son of the prophet, but he died in childhood

[2] Both Names are for the Prophet and mentioned in the Quran "And remember, Jesus, the son of Mary, said: "O Children of Israel! I am the messenger of Allah (sent) to you, confirming the Law (which came) before me, and giving Glad Tidings of a Messenger to come after me, whose name shall be Ahmad." But when he came to them with Clear Signs, they said, "this is evident sorcery!" (61:6) , "But those who believe and work deeds of righteousness, and believe in the (Revelation) sent down to Muhammad - for it is the Truth from their Lord,- He will remove from them their ills and improve their condition. "(47:2)

to whom people will be gathered on the doomsday. He is the last prophet. He is the prophet of mercy, repentance, and heroism. He is the son of Abdullah and brother of Alharith, Alzubair, Hamza, Alabbas. His epithet is (Abulfadl), as he is featured of many virtues. He is the servant of Kaaba. He is characterized of being generous.

Alhafiz Abu Omar Alnamry in his book (Alinbah Bimaarefit Qabael Alrowah) clearly stated that:

Quraish, according to the most of genealogists, belongs to Fihr ibn Malik ibn Alnadr ibn Kinanah. Being proud of their ancestry Quraish people used to warble songs.

Scholars and researchers unanimously said that Quraish is Alnadr ibn Kinanah. This was indicated by the narration mentioned by Abu Omar ibn Abdulbir, on behalf of Alashaath ibn Qais, may God be pleased with him. The narration is as follows: "I came to the Messenger of God with a delegation from Kindah, and they thought that I was the best of them. I said: 'O Messenger of God are you not from among us?' He said: 'We are the tribe of Banu Nadr ibn Kinanah, and we do not attribute ourselves to our mother and we do not deny our forefathers.'"

Alashaath ibn Qais used to say: 'If any man is brought to me who suggests that a man from Quraish does not belong to Alnadr ibn Kinanah, I would carry out the legal punishment (for slander) on him."

It was said that Quraish belongs to Elias ibn Mudhar ibn Nizar. Others said that Quraish belongs to Mudhar. These two opinions are bizarre.

For Yemeni tribes, such as Ḥimyarite, Hadramout, and Saba, they are Qahtanites, not Adnanites. Quda'a is a tribe, which is said to be Qahtanite, others said it is Adnanite. A third opinion refers that it is neither Qahtanite nor Adnanite. This opinion is bizarre, mentioned by Abu Omar and others.

This ancestry we attributed to the Adnanites is undoubtedly and unanimously proven. Scholars and genealogists agree that Adnan is one of the prophet Ishmael's decedents. Ishmael is the son of Abraham; peace be upon him. It is disagreed about how many forefathers are between. Most of the opinions go with forty forefathers, minor opinions go with seven forefathers. Some said they are nine, and others said they are fifteen. Names thereof are disagreed about.

Some ancestors and imams abhorred post-Adnanite ancestry. Malik ibn Anas Alasbahi so abhorred.

Imam Abu Omar ibn Abdulbir in his book (Alinbah), said that Adnan is son of Adad, son of Moqawem, son of Nahour, son of Tairah, son of Yaereb, son of Yashgeb, son of Nabet, son of Ishmael, son of Abraham, son of Tareh, son of Nahour, son of Sharoukh, son of Raou, son of Falikh, son of Aibar, son of Shalikh, son of Arfakheshez, son of Sam, son of Noah, son of

Lamek, son of Matoushlakh, son of Akhnokh, who is the prophet Idris, peace be upon him, he is the first prophet after Adam and Seth, he is son of Yared, son of Mahlil, son of Qainen, son of Yanish, son of Seth, son of Adam. This sequence is mentioned by Muhammed ibn Isaac ibn Yasar Almedany, the author of the Prophetic biography, and many of genealogists. In this context, Abu Alabbas Abdullah ibn Muhammed Alnashy Almutazily composed a poem, praising Prophet Muhammed, peace be upon him. It is as follows:

I am praising the Messenger of God,

to gain best of luck from the generous Prophet.

I am praising a man, of whom the utmost praising is not enough,

as his features are unprecedented.

All the Arab tribes belong to Adnan, so God said: "I do not ask you for this message any payment [but] only good will through kinship". "قُل لَّا أَسْأَلُكُمْ عَلَيْهِ أَجْرًا إِلَّا الْمَوَدَّةَ فِي الْقُرْبَى" 6:90. Ibn Abbas may God be pleased with him, said there is no one in Quraish not a relative to the Messenger of God.

These people are the elite whom God preferred. According to a narration by Muslim, on behalf of Wathla ibn Alasqaa, may God be pleased with him, the Messenger of God said: "Verily God granted eminence to Kinanah from amongst the descendants of Ishmael, and He granted eminence to Quraish amongst Kinanah, and He granted eminence to Banu Hashim amongst Quraish, and he granted me eminence from the tribe of Banu Hashim"

Israel people and their prophets belong to Abraham, peace be upon him. In his decedents, the prophecy and Torah are. God instructed them, through Moses, peace be upon him, and in Torah, according to more than a scholar interested in prophecy and prophets, that He will bring for them from their cousins a prophet, of a good word and grace. Among Ishmael's decedents, but among Adam's, there is no greater than Muhammed, peace be upon him. He said: "I am the master of the children of Adam on the Day of Judgement, and I am not boasting, not Adam nor anyone other than him, except that he will be under my banner". He also said: "I will have a rank desired by all people, even by Abraham". It is the praised rank and prestige that God promised. It is about the intercession, as he will intercede for the people, so that God will bless them on the doomsday, according to the interpretation of true narrations.

His mother is Amna, daughter of Wahb, son of Abd Manaf, son of Zuhra, son of Kilab, son of Mura.

His birth, suckling, and up-growth

The Prophet, peace be upon him, was born on Monday, in Rabie al-awwal, (the third month in the Islamic calendar), it was said on the eighth of this month, other said on the tenth. Others refer to the twelfth. Suhail ibn Bakar said, he was born in Ramadan, but this opinion is odd.

It is said he was born in Amul-Fil (the year of the elephant)[3], it is the name in Islamic history for the year approximately equating to 570 CE. Some go with that he was born later by fifty

---

[3] The name is derived from an event occurred at Mecca: Abraha, the Abyssinian, Christian ruler of Yemen, which was subject to the Kingdom of Aksum of Ethiopia, marched upon the Ka'bah in Mecca with a large army, which included one or more war elephants, intending to demolish it. However the invasion failed.

days, others said but by fifty-eight days. Some said by ten years or thirty years. Other opinions refer to forty years. But the truth is that he was born in the year of the elephant, as Ibrahim ibn Almonzir Alkhozami, Khalifa ibn Khayat, and others unanimously so said.

Prophet Muhammed's father died while he was a fetus. Some said he died several months after the Prophet's birth; others said he died a year after his birth. Other opinions refer to two years. Yet, the first opinion is the most common. He was fed in Banu Saad, as Halima Alsaadia breast-fed him. He resided there at Banu Saad for four years. He was then back to his mother, who went to Medina to visit his uncles, but she died in Al-Abwa, a village in Saudi Arabia, while she was coming from Mecca when he was only six years, three months and ten days. It was said that he was four. Imam Muslim ibn Alhagag said in his book (Sahih – that includes the true narrations of Prophet) that when the Messenger, peace be upon him, was passing by Al-Abwa on his way to Mecca, in the year of conquest of Mecca (630 AD), he asked God to visit his mother's grave, he wept and so did his troops, who were a thousand fighters.

When his mother died, he was secured by his grandpa Abdulmutlib, who died, when the Messenger was eight. He commended him to the care of his uncle, Abu Talib, as he was the brother of Abdullah, so he secured him, intensely taking care of him, and supporting him, despite he was a polytheist, till his death. Yet his support and care of the Messenger, peace be upon him, will lessen his punishment. His uncle took him to the Levant for trade, when he was twelve, as there is no one can take care of him if he was left in Mecca. His uncle and friends were noticing some signs that encourage his uncle to look after him. These signs, according to Alturmuzy, were the cloud that shadowed him and so did the tree; as well as heralding by Behira, the monk, commanding his uncle to return, so as that the Jews could not find and harm him. Again, he returned to the Levant for trade, where Khadijah bint Khuwaylid was there with her valet, Maisra, who noticed something special in Muhammed, so he returned to his mistress, informing her of what he had noticed. Thus, she was willing to get married to him, for the goodness she would have. The Messenger married her when he was twenty-five.

God was always there to protect him from the profanity of pre-Islamic epoch and of any flaw. He granted him all good morals, so he was known among his nation as the Honest, as they sensed his chastity, credibility, and honesty. When Quraish built the Kaaba when he was thirty-five, they disagreed on who would put the Black Stone; every tribe nominated itself, then they agreed that the first comer would do this. He was the Messenger of God; peace be upon him. They said: here the Honest came. He ordered them to bring a garment, to put the Stone in the midst thereof, he then ordered each tribe to hold an end of the garment, then he positioned the Stone.

Revelation

When God desired to grant His servants mercy and dignity through sending Muhammed to them, He rendered him in fond of staying alone in the void spaces, so he spent most of the time in worship in Cave of Hira. So, in Ramadan, when he was forty, he was surprised by Jibril, ordering him: "Read," he replied: "I cannot." Jibril repeated this for three times. Then, he said: "Recite in the name of your Lord who created. Created man from a clinging substance. Recite, and your Lord is the most Generous, Who taught by the pen. Taught man which he knew not." " اقْرَأْ بِاسْمِ رَبِّكَ الَّذِي خَلَقَ، خَلَقَ الْإِنْسَانَ مِنْ عَلَقٍ/ اقْرَأْ وَرَبُّكَ الْأَكْرَمُ، "الَّذِي عَلَّمَ بِالْقَلَمِ، عَلَّمَ الْإِنْسَانَ مَا لَمْ يَعْلَم 96:1-5

Then the Messenger of God, came back to his home, shivering, informing Khadija of what happened. She heralded him, saying: God will not let you down, you are keeping good relations with your kith & kin, you are honest, you are supporting others and helping them. She continued to talk about his good morals; she was his first companion.

Then he returned to the cave, but he did not witness anything. He felt depressed, but he frequently went to the cave, as he longed to the pleasantness of what he firstly witnessed. It was said that the revelation period was about two years or more. Then he was heralded that he is the Messenger of God. He was surprised by what he witnessed, fleeing to Khadija, saying: cover me.. so, God revealed: "O you who covers himself [with a garment], Arise and warn, And your Lord glorify, And your clothing purify". "يَا أَيُّهَا الْمُدَّثِّرُ، قُمْ فَأَنْذِرْ، وَرَبَّكَ فَكَبِّرْ، وَثِيَابَكَ فَطَهِّرْ" 74:1-3

The first state was about prophecy and revelation. Yet in this verse, God ordered him to warn his nation and call them to worship God. He then dedicated himself to this mission, obeying God, calling the youth and the old, the freeman and the slave, men and women, the blacks and the whites, to worship God. He found some people from every tribe, obeying him.

Abu Bakr, may God be pleased with him was his companion and so was Abdullah ibn Othman Altaimy. Abu Bakr supported the Messenger, so Othman ibn Afan, Talha, and Saad ibn Abu Waqas positively responded to Abu Bakr and obeyed the Messenger.

For Ali ibn Abu Talib, he embraced Islam when he was eight. Some said he was more than eight. Others said he embraced Islam before Abu Bakr. Anyway, his conversion to Islam is not equal to Abu Bakr's, as he was under custody of the Messenger, peace be upon him, as he was the Messenger's assistant.

Khadija and Zayd ibn Hartha also converted to Islam. The priest Warqa ibn Nofal also converted to Islam, as he believed in the Messenger. Alturmuzy narrated that the Messenger dreamt of him in a good look. The Messenger said: "I saw the priest in white clothes".

Others converted to Islam, as they got comfortable with Islam after inspection and scrutiny, yet they are harmed and punished by the fools of Mecca. God protected and preserved Muhammed, as he was under the protection of his uncle Abu Talib, he was a noble man, whom they cannot be bold or insolent with, concerning Muhammed. They know how much the Messenger is close to Abu Talib. It was God's wisdom that Abu Talib did not convert to Islam; it is to the benefit of Islam and Muhammed. The Messenger of God, peace be upon him, was spending his time praying to God, in the mornings and evenings, secretly and publicly.

Afflictions of the tortured believers and immigration to Ethiopia

When believers are instantly harmed and tortured, so they are afflicted. They were thrown into the fire, and huge rocks were put on their chests in high-temperature conditions, and if they were freed, they could not sit, because of the severe pain they suffered.

They were saying to the tortured believers that Al-Lat is your god, they replied forcibly: yes. They did so with the Geotrupidae. When Abu Jahl, Amr ibn Hashim, passed by Somaya Om Amar, while she, her husband and son were tortured, he killed her by a bayonet.

Abu Bakr, if passed by tortured slaves, bought them and then freed them, such as Bilal, his mother Hamama, Amer ibn Fuhera, Om Abs, Zinera, Alnahdiya, her daughter, and a bond-maid for Banu Oudai, who was tortured by Omar ibn Alkhatab before his conversion into Islam. His father (Abu Qahafa) told him: My son, I see you freeing weak slaves, but if you are freeing the fierce, you will be harmed. Abu Bakr replied: I seek what God wants. So, it is said that this verse is revealed in this regard: "But the righteous one will avoid it, [he] who gives [from] his wealth to purify himself" " وَسَيُجَنَّبُهَا الأَتْقَى الَّذِي يُؤْتِي مَالَهُ يَتَزَكَّى"92:17

When calamity gets worse, God allowed immigration to Ethiopia, at the west of Mecca, in-between is the Sudan desert and the sea extending from Yemen to Alkulzam. Othman ibn Afan was the first who fled to Ethiopia, accompanying his wife, Rokaia, the daughter of the Messenger. Yet, it was said that the first to flee to Ethiopia is Abu Hateb ibn Amr ibn Abd Shams ibn Abd Wed ibn Nasr ibn Malik. Then Gaefer ibn Abu Talib and some groups fled to Ethiopia; they were about eighty men. Muhammed ibn Isaac mentioned that who immigrated to Ethiopia is Abu Mousa Alashary Abdullah ibn Qais. Yet, it is said that he immigrated from Yemen to Ethiopia to Gaefer.

Immigrants preferred the kingdom of Asehama Alnajashi, who secured and treated them with generosity. There they were safe. When Quraish knew that, they sent Abdullah ibn Abu Rabia and Amr ibn Alaas, bringing gifts and antiques to Alnajashi, to hand over the immigrants, yet he refused. They let his soldiers intercede, but again he refused. They rumored that the immigrants are defaming Jesus, saying that he is a slave. So, Alnajashi associated with the Muslims presided by Gaefer ibn Abu Talib, may God be pleased with him. He said: Quraish is claiming that you are defaming Jesus? Gaefer recited the Surah of Maryam. So, Alnajashi took a rod from the ground, saying: this is the same mentioned in Bible. Go, you are safe on my land. Then he told Amr ibn Alaas and Abdullah: If you gave me a mountain of gold, I will not handover the immigrants to you. He gave them back their gifts. Both men returning Quraish hitting   the   ceiling.

Quraish boycotting Banu Hashim and Banu Almutlib

Hamza, uncle of the Messenger of God, peace be upon him, and many people converted to Islam. So, Islam spread and prevailed.

This infuriated Quraish, as they agreed to boycott Banu Hashim and Banu Almutlib, of Abd Manaf; they agreed not to pledge allegiance to them, not to marry them, not to talk to them and not to associate with them, unless they handover the Messenger of God, peace be upon him. In this regard, a leaf was written, and attached to the Kaaba. It is said that Mansour ibn Akrama ibn Amer ibn Hashim ibn Abd Manaf. It is said that Alnadr ibn Alharith is who wrote such leaf, the Messenger of

God, peace be upon him, invoked God to take revenge from Al-nadr, so his hand got paralyzed.

People, believers, and disbelievers, supported Banu Hashim and Banu Almutlib, but Abu Lahab, God curse him, supported Quraish, who kept boycotting Banu Hashim and Banu Almutlib for three years.

Some people from Quraish sought to nullify this leaf, and it was Hisham ibn Amr ibn Rabia ibn Alharith ibn Hubaib ibn Gazima ibn Malik ibn Hisl ibn Amer ibn Loai, who took the responsibility of such matter. The Messenger of God, peace be upon him, informed his nation, that God had sent white ants to eat all of it, except God's name.

Thereafter, Banu Hashim and Banu Almutlib returned to Mecca, where reconciliation was held, in spite of Abu Jahl.

News reached the immigrants in Ethiopia that some of Quraish people have converted to Islam, so some of them returned to Mecca, but they found calamity and torture as before, they stayed in Mecca till they immigrated to Medina, except Al-sakran ibn Amr, husband of Suda bint Zamaa, who died after returning from Ethiopia before immigration to Medina. Salma ibn Hisham and Ayash ibn Abu Rabia, did not go to Medina, they were detained. Abdullah ibn Makhrama ibn Aloza was detained, and on the battle day of Badr, he fled from the disbelievers to the Muslims.

The departure of the Prophet to Taif

When the leaf was nullified, it was the death of Khadija, may God be pleased with her and death of Abu Talib, only three days were in between. So, the Messenger of God, peace be upon him, suffered a big calamity, he moved to Taif to seek refugee there and get their assistance. He called them to worship God, but they did not respond, and aggressively harmed him.

He left them and entered Mecca, at Almotem ibn Oudai ibn Nofal ibn Abd Manaf, calling them to worship God. Altufail ibn Amr Aldawsy converted to Islam, whom the Messenger of God asked God to grant him a remarkable sign, so he was granted light in his face. Altufail told the Messenger of God: I am afraid that it is said to be body mutilation, so the Messenger asked God to respond, the light shifted to his whip. He is known for the light emitting from him. He called his people to worship

God, some of them converted to Islam. When the Messenger reached Khaibar, the new Muslims resided in approximately eight houses.

Muhammed's night journey to Jerusalem and midnight ascent to Heaven

The Messenger of God, peace be upon him, according to the true narrations by his companions and scholars, was taken from Alharam mosque to Jerusalem, on the Buraq (a steed), accompanied by Jibril, peace be upon him. Then he led the prophets praying at Alaqsa mosque in Jerusalem.

Then he ascended to the Heaven gradually, till he reached the seventh Heaven, he knew the ranks of the prophets there. Then the Buraq took him to Sidrat Almuntaha, a Lote tree that marks the end of the Seventh Heaven, where he saw Jibril as

God created him. On this day, God instructed him about the five prayers.

Scholars disagree whether he saw God or not. There are two opinions:

Ibn Abbas said the Messenger, peace be upon him, saw God, yet he was quoted saying that the Messenger felt the existence of God.

In both Sahih books, Aisha, may God be pleased with her, denied this. She and ibn Masoud said that the Messenger saw Jibril.

Imam Muslim in his Sahih, according to Qatada, on behalf of Abdullah ibn Shaqiq, and Abu Zar, narrated: "I asked the Messenger of God: Did you see thy Lord? He said: (He is) Light; how could I see Him?". In another narration, he said: "I saw Light." This narration is enough for this matter.

When the Messenger of God is back to his nation, he told them about the great wonders the God showed him, so they continued to accuse him of lying, harm and be bold with him.

He continued to call people to God. Yet, his uncle, Abu Lahab was telling people not to believe him, accusing him of being a liar. Arabs were mistreating him, as they were hearing Quraish saying: he is a liar, a magician, a clergyman, a poet... They were accusing him of lying, without any inspection or scrutiny. Only the wise, when listening to him and recognizing his words, witnessed that he is right and converted to Islam.

CHAPTER 9

First and second treaties of Alaqba

The Messenger of God, peace be upon him, met some of Ansar at Alaqba, all of them belong to Khazraj; Abu Omama Asaad ibn Zirara ibn Ads, Ouf ibn Alharith ibn Rifaa, Rafe ibn Malik ibn Alajlan, Qoutba ibn Amer ibn Hadida, Aqba ibn Amer ibn Nabi and Jabir ibn Abdullah ibn Riaab. The Messenger of God, peace be upon him, called them to Islam. They converted to Islam, then returned to Medina, calling to Islam there, so it spread and prevailed so that all houses in Medina are encompassing Islam.

In the next year, twelve men of them came; the first six except for Jabir ibn Abdullah ibn Riaab, among them are Moaz ibn Alharith, brother of Ouf Almotqadem, Thaqwan ibn Abd Qais ibn Khalda, who resided in Mecca till moved to Medina – it is said that he is an Immigrant belonging to Ansar – Obada ibn Alsamet ibn Qais, Abu Abdulrahman Yazid ibn Thaalba. These are ten of Khazraj and two of Aws; Abulhaitham Malik ibn Altayhan and Owim ibn Saada. All of them pledged allegiance to the Messenger of God, peace be upon him.

When they moved to Medina, the Messenger of God, peace be upon him, sent with them Amr ibn Om Maktoum and Mosaab ibn Omair, to teach the new Muslims Qur'an. Through them, many of them converted to Islam, who are Osaid ibn Hodair and Saad ibn Moaz. Upon their conversion to Islam, all people of Abd Alashhal, men and women so did, except Amr ibn Thabet ibn Waqsh who converted to Islam on the day of Battle of Uhud, he took part in the battle, and was killed, before kneeling worshipping God. The Messenger of God was informed about him; he said: "He acted less and was awarded much."

Islam spread and prevailed in Medina. Mosaab returned to Mecca. In that year, there were a lot of Ansar (Muslims and non-Muslims) and the leader Albaraa ibn Marur, may God be pleased with him, went on pilgrimage.

At the first third of the night at which the treaty of Alaqba was concluded, seventy-three men and women went to the Messenger, sneaking to pledge allegiance to him, they tried to hide from their nation and disbelievers of Mecca. The first who pledged allegiance to the Messenger was Albaraa ibn Marur; he was the one initiating to goodness, as he concluded the treaty.

Alabbas, the Messenger's uncle was present, to witness the conclusion of the treaty, although he was following his nation's religion.

At that night, the Messenger of God, peace be upon him, chose twelve heads; Asaad ibn Zirara ibn Ads, Saad ibn Alrabie ibn Amr, Abdullah ibn Rawaha ibn Thaalba ibn Imru Alqais, Rafe ibn Malik ibn Alajlan, Albaraa ibn Marur ibn Sakhr ibn Khansaa, Abdullah ibn Amr ibn Haram, father of Jabir, who converted to Islam that night, Saad ibn Obada ibn Dulim, Almonther ibn Amr ibn Khonais and Obada ibn Alsamet. These are nine from Khazraj. From Aws, there were three, Osaid ibn Alhodair ibn Simak, Saad ibn Khaithma ibn Alharith and Rifaa ibn Abdulmonther ibn Zubair.

The two women were Om Omara Nisiba bint Kaab ibn Amr, her son Musailama killed Habib ibn Zaid ibn Assem ibn Kaab and Asmaa bint Amr ibn Oudai ibn Nabi.

On conclusion of the treaty, they asked the Messenger of God, peace be upon him to go to the people of Alaqba, but he refused, he later allowed the Muslims in Mecca to move to Medina. The first Meccan who did so were Abu Salma ibn Abd Alasad and his wife, whose father hindered her to go with her husband for a year, then she went to Medina, with her son, helped by Othman ibn Talha. It is said that Abu Salma immigrated before the last treaty of Alaqba. Then the groups moved consecutively.

CHAPTER 10

Migration of the Prophet

Muslims existed there in Mecca at that time were the Messenger, Abu Bakr, and Ali ibn Abu Talib, may God be pleased with both of them, as well as some who were detained by the disbelievers. Abu Bakr packed his and the Messenger's luggage only waiting God to order the Messenger to move. The disbelievers intended to murder the Messenger and let the killers stand in front of his house's door, to kill him once he came out. But when he came out, nobody saw him. According to a narration by the Messenger of God, he put some sand on each one's head, then moved to Abu Bakr's house. Then at night, they came out through a wicket in Abu Bakr's house. They hired Abdullah ibn Urayqat, a skilled guide, to help them reaching Medina. They trusted him, although he was following his nation's religion. They waited for him at cave of Thawr (a famous cave in a mountain in Mecca), and on reaching there, God misguided Quraish, so they did not know where Muhammed and Abu Bakr are.

Amer ibn Fuhera was meeting Abu Bakr there, and Asmaa, daughter of Abu Bakr, was bringing them food there. Abdullah ibn Abu Bakr was reporting the news in Mecca, so they can be cautious. When the disbelievers reached Thawr, they saw the spider web covering the opening of the cave and two pigeons sitting there. This is an interpretation of the following God's words: "If you do not aid the Prophet - God has already aided him when those who disbelieved had driven him out [of Makkah] as one of two, when they were in the cave, and he said to his companion, "Do not grieve; indeed God is with us." And God sent down his tranquility upon him and supported him with angels you did not see and made the word of those who disbelieved the lowest, while the word of God - that is the highest. And God is Exalted in Might and Wise." " إِلَّا تَنصُرُوهُ فَقَدْ نَصَرَهُ اللَّهُ إِذْ أَخْرَجَهُ الَّذِينَ كَفَرُوا ثَانِيَ اثْنَيْنِ إِذْ هُمَا فِي الْغَارِ إِذْ يَقُولُ لِصَاحِبِهِ لَا تَحْزَنْ إِنَّ اللَّهَ مَعَنَا ۖ فَأَنزَلَ اللَّهُ سَكِينَتَهُ عَلَيْهِ وَأَيَّدَهُ بِجُنُودٍ لَّمْ تَرَوْهَا وَجَعَلَ كَلِمَةَ الَّذِينَ كَفَرُوا السُّفْلَىٰ ۗ وَكَلِمَةُ اللَّهِ هِيَ الْعُلْيَا ۗ وَاللَّهُ عَزِيزٌ حَكِيمٌ" At-Tawba 9:40

When the disbelievers were there, Abu Bakr said: "If any of them should look under his feet, he would see us." The Prophet said, "O Abu Bakr! What do you think of two (persons) the third of whom is God?"

After three days, ibn Urayqat arrived bringing two camels. Abu Bakr followed Amer ibn Fuhera. Ibn Urayqat guided them, on his camel.

Quraish announced a reward of 100 camels for anyone who tracked Muhammad and Abu Bakr. When Muhammed and Abu Bakr passed by Mudlaj, Suraqah ibn Malik witnessed them and tracked them. When he came close to them, he heard the Messenger reciting Qur'an, while Abu Bakr was looking around, worrying about the Messenger, telling him: O' Messenger, here is Suraqah ibn Malik seeing us.

The Messenger asked God to protect them from him, so limbs of his steed sank in the sands. He said: I am getting injured, ask God to save me and I will protect you from Quraish. The Messenger asked God to save him; then God freed Suraqah. He asked the Messenger to write a message, and Abu Bakr did so. Then he returned and converted to Islam in the year of the farewell pilgrimage.

The Messenger then passed by tent of Om Maabad (Aateka bint Khalid), who felt the signs of his prophecy as her sheep produced much milk in a year when everything was barren.

The Prophet's arrival at Medina

Ansar were informed that Muhammed left Mecca and on his way to Medina, so they were going daily to Harrah waiting for him. On this Monday, 12 of Rabie al-awwal, in the thirteenth year of his prophecy, the Messenger arrived at Medina. The first who saw him was a Jewish man, who called: O' Banu Qaila (Aws and Khazraj), here is your grandfather whom you are waiting. Thus, Ansar came armed to salute him for prophecy.

He stayed in Qubaa (a neighborhood in Medina) at Kolthoum ibn Alhadm, it is said but at Saad ibn Khaythama. Muslims came in groups to salute the Messenger. Some or most of them falsely thought that Abu Bakr is Muhammed for his white hair. When it got hotter, Abu Bakr stood to shadow the Messenger with his garment, then people recognized which is the Messenger.

The Prophet accommodation in Medina

The Messenger stayed in Qubaa for several days. It is said that the Prophet stayed there for fourteen days while he was founding Qubaa mosque. Then he moved to be at Banu Salim ibn Ouf on Friday, so he performed the Friday prayer in the mosque located in Ranonaa valley. Household of Banu Salim wanted the Messenger to stay in their house, but he said that his camel is ordered to continue its way. Its camel was walking passing by all Ansar houses who all desired him to stay at their houses. When it reached the place, where his mosque was later built, it knelt down, he descended and stayed in the house of Banu Alnajar, so Abu Ayoub carried the luggage of the Messenger to his house.

Later, he purchased the land on which his mosque was built; it was a place where two orphans were drying dates. He built a mosque there and some rooms for his family.

Ali, may God be pleased with him, stayed in Mecca till returning the trusts that were at the Messenger's, then followed him to Medina.

The bond between the immigrants and Ansar

The Messenger made peace with Jews in Medina and made a pact in this regard. Their rabbi, Abdullah ibn Salam, may God be pleased with him converted to Islam. The disbelievers were three tribes: Banu Qaynuqa, Banu Nadir and Banu Qurayza.

The messenger created a bond between the immigrants and Ansar; it was based on the kinship. Zakat (The obligatory tax that every Muslim must give) was imposed by God to help the poor immigrants. This was stated by ibn Hazm.

The duty of Jihad (striving in the path of God)

When the Messenger resided in Medina, supported by Ansar who protected and secured him. All the Arabs started to punish them. God were allowing Muslims to strive in the path of God in Surah of Al-Haj, a Meccan one – *"Permission [to fight] has been given to those who are being fought, because they were wronged. And indeed, God is competent to give them victory." "*

22:39 أُذِنَ لِلَّذِينَ يُقَاتَلُونَ بِأَنَّهُمْ ظُلِمُوا ۚ وَإِنَّ اللَّهَ عَلَىٰ نَصْرِهِمْ لَقَدِيرٌ "

Then when Muslims became stronger in Medina, God said in Surah of Al-Baqrah: *"Fighting has been enjoined upon you while it is hateful to you. But perhaps you hate a thing, and it is good for you, and perhaps you love a thing, and it is bad for you. And God Knows, while you know not."* *كُتِبَ عَلَيْكُمُ الْقِتَالُ وَهُوَ "*

كُرْهٌ لَكُمْ ۖ وَعَسَىٰ أَن تَكْرَهُوا شَيْئًا وَهُوَ خَيْرٌ لَّكُمْ ۖ وَعَسَىٰ أَن تُحِبُّوا شَيْئًا وَهُوَ شَرٌّ لَّكُمْ ۗ وَاللَّهُ يَعْلَمُ وَأَنتُمْ لَا تَعْلَمُونَ" 2:216

Expedition of Al-Abwa

Expedition of Al-Abwa was the first for the Messenger, peace be upon him, it was in Safar (second month of the Islamic calendar) 2 AH, as the Messenger went himself till he reached Waddan, so he made peace with Banu Damra ibn Bakr ibn Abd Monat ibn Kinanah, presided by Makhsi ibn Amr, then he returned to Medina and did not fight, assigning Saad ibn Obada, may God be pleased with him as a guardian there.

Mission of Hamza ibn Abdulmutlib

His uncle, Hamza, may God be pleased with him, was sent along with thirty travelers, not including any of Ansar, to Seif Albahr, but he met Abu Jahl, and about thirty individuals went with him. Majdi ibn Amr Algahny settled the matter, as he was neutral.

The mission of Obaida ibn Alhareth ibn Abdulmutlib

Obaida ibn Alhareth ibn Abdulmutlib was sent in Rabie al-akhar (the fourth month in the Islamic calendar) among sixty or eighty travelers of the immigrants to Hijaz. They met a great crowd of

Quraish, presided by Akrama ibn Abu Jahl. It is said that the crowd was presided by Mikraz ibn Hafs, but they did not fight. Saad ibn Abu Waqas only threw an arrow towards them, so it was the first arrow thrown, striving in the path to God. Almaqdad ibn Amr Alkandy and Otba ibn Ghathwan, may God be pleased with them, fled from the disbelievers to the Muslims.

Expedition of Buwat

Then the Messenger of God, peace be upon him, launched the expedition of Buwat. He himself went in Rabie al-alkhar, 2 AH. Alsaib ibn Othman ibn Madhun, was accompanied in this battle, who took the way till he reached Buwat from Radwa, he came back with no war.

Expedition of Alushairah

Then it was the expedition of Alushairah. The Messenger himself went in Jumada al-awal (fifth month of the Islamic calendar) to Alushairah, it is a place in midst of Yanbu, where the Messenger stayed there for the rest of the month and for some days of Ju-mada al-akhar (sixth month of the Islamic calendar), he made peace with Banu Mudlaj, he returned with no war to fight in or a gyp to avoid. He assigned Abu Salma ibn Abd Alasad as a guardian there. Imam Muslim mentioned in his Sahih, according to a narration by Abu Isaac Alsubeie who said: "I asked Zaid: how many battles (expeditions) the Messenger launched? He replied: "nineteen, first of them is Alushairah".

First battle of Badr

Ten days later, the Messenger went to Badr, as Kurz ibn Jabir Alfihri, had raided the manor of Medina. He called Kurz and when reached a valley called Safwan, near Badr, he returned, and the Messenger assigned Zaid ibn Haritha as a guardian.
He sent Saad ibn Waqas, may God be pleased with him to bring Kurz ibn Jabir. Yet, it was said that Saad was sent for another end.

Mission of Abdullah ibn Gahsh

Then the Messenger of God, peace be upon him, sent Abdullah ibn Gahsh ibn Riaab Alasdi along with eight immigrants, he wrote a message for him and ordered him not to look at, but after two days. When Abdullah opened the message after two days, it was: "if you are reading my message, so go on your way till you reach Nakhla between Mecca and Taif and watch Quraish there to know about them". Abdullah obeyed and informed his companions of that; telling them that the mission is not obligatory, according to the Messenger's orders, whoever seeks martyrdom can go on and who fears death can return, for me I am going on. So, all of them went on.

On their way, Saad ibn Abu Waqas and Otba ibn Ghazwan lost the camels they were tracing, so they failed to track Kurz. Abdullah ibn Gahsh proceeded till he reached Nakhla, he was passed by camels belonging to Quraish, carrying raisin, food and trading, having Amr ibn Alhadremy, Othman ibn Abdullah ibn Almoghayra, Nofal ibn Abdullah ibn Almoghayra and Alhakam ibn Kisan Mola ibn Almoghayra. Muslims were discussing that they are on the last day of Rajab (seventh month of the Islamic calendar), so if the Muslims battled them, it is a violation in the months God prohibited fight in, and if the Muslims let them flee, they would enter the Haram. Eventually, they agreed to meet them, one threw an arrow at Amr ibn Alhadremy, so he died. Othman and Alhakam were seized, Nofal was released.

They took the camels, it was the first booty in Islam, the first Khums (20% tax that must be paid on all items regarded as ghanima, which is booty seized at war), it was the first murdered and the first prisoner in Islam, yet the Messenger denounced what they did.

Quraish turned to be more intolerant, saying that Muhammed allowed what it is prohibited by Islam, so God revealed: "They ask you about the sacred month - about fighting therein. Say, "Fighting therein is great [sin], but averting [people] from the way of God and disbelief in Him and [preventing access to] Alharam mosque and the expulsion of its people therefrom are greater [evil] in the sight of God." " يَسْأَلُونَكَ عَنِ الشَّهْرِ الْحَرَامِ قِتَالٍ فِيهِ ۖ قُلْ قِتَالٌ فِيهِ كَبِيرٌ ۖ وَصَدٌّ عَن سَبِيلِ اللَّهِ وَكُفْرٌ بِهِ وَالْمَسْجِدِ الْحَرَامِ وَإِخْرَاجُ أَهْلِهِ مِنْهُ أَكْبَرُ عِندَ اللَّهِ" 2:217

This means it is true that fight in Haram months (sacred) is prohibited in Islam, but the actions of Quraish (disbelief of God and Alharam mosque as well as expelling of Muhammed and his companions who are the folks of the mosque) are of much significance for God.

The Messenger of God, peace be upon him, accepted the Khums of this booty and received the blood money for Othman and Alhakam.

Change of Qiblah and the duty of fasting

Expedition of Al-Abwa was the first for the Messenger, peace be upon him, it was in Safar (second month of the Islamic calendar) 2 AH, as the Messenger went himself till he reached Waddan, so he made peace with Banu Damra ibn Bakr ibn Abd Monat ibn Kinanah, presided by Makhsi ibn Amr, then he returned to Medina and did not fight, assigning Saad ibn Obada, may God be pleased with him as a guardian there.

Great Battle of Badr

It is the great event when God showed how right should be, supported Islam and confuted blasphemy and disbelievers. As in Ramadan (the ninth month of the Islamic calendar), the Messenger was informed that there is a caravan coming from the Levant with Abu Sufian Sakhr ibn Harb, and forty-three men of Quraish, carrying a lot of money to Qurasih. So, the Messenger called the people to go there. Then he left Medina in Ramadan, assigning ibn Om Maktoum as a guardian. When he was in Arrawhaa, he ordered Abu Lubaba ibn Abd Almonzir to guard Medina, but he has no horses but Alzubair's and Almiqdad ibn Alaswad Alkindy's steed and seventy camels, while the one camel is carrying more than two or three men. The Messenger, Ali and Marthad ibn Abu Marthad Alghanwy were on a camel. Zaid ibn Haritha, (Ansa and Abu Kabsha), the valets of the Messenger and Hamza were on a camel. Abu Bakr, Omar and Abdulrahman ibn Ouf were on another... and so on.

Banner was given by the Messenger, peace be upon him, to Mosaab ibn Omair. The first flag was given to Ali ibn Abu Talib, the second one to a man from Ansar. The Ansar flag was given to Saad ibn Moaz. At the rear of the patrol was Qais ibn Abu Saasaa. When they were near Alsafra (a village in Medina), the Messenger sent Basbas ibn Amr Algahny, an ally of Banu Saada and Oudai ibn Abu Alzaghbaa, an ally of Banu Alnajar to Badr, to hunt for news about the caravan.

For Abu Sufian, he was informed that the Messenger, peace be upon him, is on his way to him, so he hired Damdam ibn Amr Alghafary to go to Mecca calling Quraish for help, in order to protect their caravan from Muhammed and his Companions.

Call for help reached Mecca people, so they rushed, except Abu Lahb, gathering the Arab tribes, but only Banu Oudai did not respond to Quarish.

They rushed as God said of them: "And do not be like those who came forth from their homes insolently and to be seen by people and avert [them] from the way of God. And God is encompassing of what they do". " بَطَرًا وَرِئَاءَ النَّاسِ وَيَصُدُّونَ عَن سَبِيلِ اللَّه" 8:47

They were full of rage and wrath at the Messenger and his companions as they wanted to take their caravan, and previously attacked Amr ibn Alhadremy and his caravan.

So, God gathered them on a non-date, as he said: "If you had made an appointment [to meet], you would have missed the appointment. But [it was] so that God might accomplish a matter already destined"'" وَلَوْ تَوَاعَدتُّمْ لَاخْتَلَفْتُمْ فِي الْمِيعَادِ ۚ وَلَٰكِن لِّيَقْضِيَ اللَّهُ أَمْرًا "كَانَ مَفْعُولًا" 8:42

When the Messenger knew about that Quraish people had rushed, he consulted his companions, the immigrants and Ansar. Saad ibn Moaz said: "O' Messenger, it seems to be risky, but if you want us to cross the sea, we will, so we agree. The Messenger ordered the patrol to move.

Then the Messenger reached a place near Badr and went with one of his companions, requiring information about Quraish, then left. At night, he sent Ali, Saad and Alzubair to Badr, hunting for news. They returned brining two of Quraish servants, when the Messenger was performing his prayer. He asked them: "To whom are you?" They said: we are sommeliers for Quraish. The Messenger wished that the caravan of Abu Sufian would be close to take it as a booty, because fighting Quraish is risker, as they are tough and well-equipped for wars. The Messenger asked them about the place of Quraish, they informed him that they are behind dune. He asked them how many Quraish people are? They said: we do not know. He asked about how many sheep they slaughtered daily. They said: ten on one day and nine on another. He said: so, they are nine-hundreds to a thousand.

For Basbas and Oudai, they reached Badr. They heard a bondmaid saying for another, will not you give me back my money? She replied: I will when the caravan arrived tomorrow or after tomorrow. They rushed after what they heard, followed by Abu Sufian. He asked Majdi ibn Amr: Did you notice any of Muhammed's companions? He replied: No, but there are two travelers stopped at this hill. Abu Sufian hurtled to their place. He took their camels and found seeds, recognizing that these seeds belong to Medina, so he redirected to the coast and survived, then he sent to Quraish informing them about his and the caravan's survival and ordering them to return.

Quraish knew about this, but Abu Jahl refused to obey, saying: we will not return till we reach Badr to stay there for three days, drinking wine and listening to chanteuses, so that the Arabs will fear us. Alakhnas ibn Shariq returned to his nation, Banu Zuhra, saying: you raced to protect your caravan and it is safe. No one reached Badr, except uncles of Muslim ibn Obaidallah ibn Abdullha ibn Shihab ibn Abdullah, father of Alzuhry, as they reached the battle and died as disbelievers.

The Messenger, peace be upon him, wanted to reach before Quraish. Alhabab ibn Almonther ibn Amr said: "O' Messenger of God, are you ordered by God to stop there or you did so for war and subterfuge? He said: for war and subterfuge. Alhabab said: but it is not a suitable stop, let us reach the nearest waterbody and buried wills we left behind and then build a sink, so we can drink but they cannot. The Messenger found the idea sound, so God prevented Quraish from the water through heavy rains. It was a malice of the disbelievers and a blessing for the Muslims.

The Messenger walked in the place of the battle, showing them the death of these people one by one, saying here this will die and there that will die. Abdullah ibn Masoud: I swear that he was right with all places he referred to.

The Messenger was praying at this night near a tree root. It was Friday, 17th Ramadan. When Quraish arrived in troops, he said: "O' God, here is the proud and haughty Quraish challenging you and your Messenger". Haki, ibn Hizam and Otba ibn Rabia suggested that Quraish could return to avoid battling, but Abu Jahl so refused. He ordered brother of Amr ibn Alhadremy to kill Amr. He shouted: O' Amr! So, the battle broke out.

The Messenger reorganized the troops and returned with Abu Bakr to Alarish. Saad ibn Moaz and some of Ansar stood at Alarish to protect the Messenger.

Otba ibn Rabia, Sheba ibn Rabia and Alwalid ibn Otba rushed to quarrel. So, three Ansar Muslims met them (Ouf ibn Afraa, Maouz ibn Afraa and Abdulla ibn Rawaha. They asked: who are you? They replied: Ansar. They said: You are known for your nobility, but we want our cousins. So, Ali ibn Alharith, Obaida ibn Alharith and Hamza appeared. Ali killed Alwalid. Hamza killed Otba, it was said that Hamza killed Sheba too. Obaida was injured and died in Alsafraa. According to Sahih, Ali, may God be pleased with him interpreted this verse: "These are two adversaries who have disputed over their Lord" in battle of Badr. "هَٰذَانِ خَصْمَانِ اخْتَصَمُوا فِي رَبِّهِم" **22:19** Yet, undoubtedly, this is a verse in Surah of Al-Haj, it is Meccan, battle of Badr was after it. Yet the quarrel is included in the meaning of the verse.

The battle became severe and quarrels became brutal. The Messenger worked on invocation, as the victory was granted by God. Abu Bakr was assuring the Messenger, who was saying: "O' God, perish this gang". In this regard, God's words correspond: "[Remember] when you asked help of your Lord, and He answered you, "Indeed, I will reinforce you with a thousand from the angels, following one another." " إِذْ تَسْتَغِيثُونَ رَبَّكُمْ فَاسْتَجَابَ "لَكُمْ أَنِّي مُمِدُّكُم بِأَلْفٍ مِّنَ الْمَلَائِكَةِ مُرْدِفِينَ" 8:9 The Messenger had a quick nap, then got up saying: "O' Abu Bakr, rejoice, here is Jibril is full of dust"

Satan appeared for Quraish in the look of Suraqa ibn Malik, leader of Mudlaj, to support them, convincing them of what they were doing, as they feared Banu Mudlaj to take their money. In this regard, God's words are as follows: "And [remember] when Satan made their deeds pleasing to them and said, "No one can overcome you today from among the people, and indeed, I am your protector." But when the two armies sighted each other, he turned on his heels and said, "Indeed, I am disassociated from you. Indeed, I see what you do not see; indeed I fear God." " وَإِذْ زَيَّنَ لَهُمُ الشَّيْطَانُ أَعْمَالَهُمْ وَقَالَ لَا غَالِبَ لَكُمُ الْيَوْمَ مِنَ النَّاسِ وَإِنِّي جَارٌ لَّكُمْ فَلَمَّا تَرَاءَتِ الْفِئَتَانِ نَكَصَ عَلَىٰ عَقِبَيْهِ وَقَالَ إِنِّي بَرِيءٌ مِّنكُمْ إِنِّي أَرَىٰ مَا لَا تَرَوْنَ" 8:48

Angels were sent by God to support Muslims and kill disbelievers. The first who fled were Khalid ibn Alalam, but he was
caught and seized. Muslims were tracing the disbelievers, killing
seventy and seizing seventy. They took their booties. One of the
murdered disbelievers whom the Messenger named was Abu
Jahl, killed by Amr ibn Aljomouh, Maouz ibn Afraa and Abdullah ibn Masoud, who beheaded him. For bodies of Otba ibn
Rabia, Sheba ibn Rabia, Alwalid ibn Otba and Omia ibn Khalaf,
the Messenger ordered them to get them back to the wills. He
blamed them saying: "You were the worst members of the tribe,
you accused me of lying while others believed me, you let me
down, while others supported me, you expelled me while others
secured me. He stayed in Badr yard for three days.

Then he migrated taking the captives and booties, under care
of Abdullah ibn Kaab ibn Amr Alnajary. In battle of Badr, God
revealed the Surah of Alanfal. When he reached Alsafraa, he
distributed the booties, according to God's instructions. He ordered to kill Alnadr ibn Alharith, he was abusive to the
Messenger. His sister lamented him, and an elegiac poetry was
composed, they claim that when the Messenger heard such poetry said: "If I had heard it before killing him, I would not have
done so". When he stopped at Araq Alzibia, he ordered to kill
Oqba ibn Abu Muaiat, who was also killed.

The Messenger consulted his companions regarding captives:
"what we shall do with them?" Omar ibn Alkhatab suggested
that they should be killed. Abu Bakr suggested a blood money

per head. The Messenger preferred Abu Bakr's opinion. God faintly blamed the Prophet for such act in His words: "It is not for a prophet to have captives [of war] until he inflicts a massacre [upon God's enemies] in the land. Some Muslims desire the commodities of this world, but God desires [for you] the Hereafter. And God is Exalted in Might and Wise." " مَا كَانَ لِنَبِيٍّ أَن يَكُونَ لَهُ أَسْرَىٰ حَتَّىٰ يُثْخِنَ فِي الْأَرْضِ ۚ تُرِيدُونَ عَرَضَ الدُّنْيَا وَاللَّهُ يُرِيدُ الْآخِرَةَ ۗ وَاللَّهُ عَزِيزٌ حَكِيمٌ" 8:67

Imam Muslim in his Sahih, according to ibn Abbas, mentioned a long Hadith (narration) by the Messenger in this regard, as he set the blood money to be four hundred dirhams.

The Messenger was back to Medina, supported and triumphant. Then, many of Medina people converted to Islam, Abdullah ibn Abu ibn Saloul and his group of hypocrites converted to Islam, seeking protection.

Troops of Badr

Troops of Badr included about three-hundred men: eighty-six men of immigrants, sixty-one from Aws and a hundred and seventy from Khazraj.

Aws men were less those of Khazraj, despite their power and force in battle, because their houses were in the farthest parts of city, so when they were called, it was easier for Khazraj to go, because their houses were nearer. Scholars of battles and biographies disagreed about Badr troops.

The disbelievers were nine-hundreds to a thousand, as the Messenger, peace be upon him, said.

Fourteen Muslims were killed; six immigrants, six from Khazraj and two from Aws.

The first martyr was Mahgaa, valet of Omar ibn Alkhatab, a man from Ansar said he is called Haritha ibn Suraqa.
Seventy disbelievers were killed. Some said but less than seventy. Captives were also seventy. The Messenger settled the matter of Badr and captives in Shawal (the tenth month of the Islamic calendar)

Expedition of Banu Salim

After seven days, he directed to Banu Salim, he resided there for three days and returned with no quarrel. He assigned Sibaa ibn Orfuta as a guardian for Medina. It is said but ibn Om Maktoum was the guardian.

Expedition of Sawiq

When Abu Sufian returned to Mecca and known about the result of battle of Badr, he vowed that he would not rest till he attacked the Messenger, so he went with two-hundred people, and stopped at Alaridh and stayed for one night at Banu Nadir, with Salam ibn Mishkam. He became a friend of him and killed a man from Ansar.

The Messenger was informed of what happened, he and Muslims traced him, reaching Qarqara Alkudr, and did not get Abu Sufian and the disbelievers, leaving many of their food including Sawiq (fine flour), so the expedition is called Sawiq. It was in Zulhija (the twelfth and last month in the Islamic calendar), then he returned to Medina, that he left under the guardianship of Abu Lubaba.

Expedition of Zu Amar

The Messenger, peace be upon him, paused his expeditions for the rest of Zulhija, then invaded Najd, targeting Ghatafan, leaving Othman ibn Afan as a guardian of Medina. So, he stayed in Najd for the whole month of Safar and returned with no war.

Expedition of Buhran

The Messenger was targeting Quraish in Rabie al-akhar, assign-ing ibn Om Maktoum as a guardian in Medina. The Messenger reached Buhran, then he returned with no war.

Siege of Banu Qaynuqa

Banu Qaynuqa, breached the promise, they were tradesmen and jewelers, about seven-hundred fighters. The Messenger moved to siege them, leaving Beshir ibn Abd Almonzir in Medina. He managed to do so for fifteen days. Abdullah ibn Abu ibn Saloul, the leader of Khazraj interceded, as they were allies of Khazraj. The Messenger accepted to release them, then they left Medina.

Murder of Kaab ibn Alashraf

The Jewish Kaab ibn Alasharf was from Tayy and his mother was from Banu Nadir, he was harming the Messenger and the believers and courting wives of the believers. After the battle of Badr, he went to Mecca urging people against the Messenger and the believers, so the Messenger ordered the Muslims to kill him; saying: who will kill Kaab ibn Alashraf, he harmed God and his Messenger? Men from Ansar and Aws were called: Muhammed ibn Muslima, Abbad ibn Bishr ibn Waqsh, Abu Naila (Silkan ibn Salama ibn Waqsh, foster-brother of Kaab ibn Alashraf, Alharith ibn Aws ibn Moaz and Abu Abs ibn Gabr. The Messenger allowed them to say whatever they want to deceive him. So, they went to him, deluding him. So, he felt safe and they managed to kill him. Then they returned to the Messenger who was praying at a full-moon night. He asked God the best for them. Alharith had some wounds, on which the Messenger spat, so they were healed. Jews started to discuss how to kill the Messenger, so he allowed his followers to kill the Jews.

Battle of Uhud

Through the battle of Uhud, God examined His servants who believe in Him to differentiate between the true believers and the hypocrites. When Quraish's elite were killed in Badr and witnessed an unexpected disaster, Abu Sufian ibn Harab presided the tribe, because they lost all their leaders and moved to the borders of the city, but he did not get what he wanted, then he started to call Quraish and urge them to kill the Muslims and the Messenger, so he managed to gather three-thousand men of Quraish, allies and Alahabish (according to Mount Hubshi). Later, he moved with his troops towards Medina and stooped near Mount Uhud, at a place called Aynin, in Shawal, 3 AH.

The Messenger consulted his companions: shall he move out to encounter them or stay in Medina? Some who missed battle of Badr referred insisting that Muslims should move out. Abdullah ibn Abu ibn Saloul and others suggested staying in Medina.

After insisting by the first group, the Messenger went to be armored. Some of them dampened saying; "O' Messenger, if you want to stay in Medina, so do." He replied: "if a prophet gets armored, he shall not stay far from the battle". He left ibn Om Maktoum as a guardian in Medina.

He went out with a thousand fighters. On their way, Abdullah ibn Abu Saloul returned with three-hundred fighters to Medina, they are then followed by Abdullah ibn Amr ibn Haram, father of Jabir, may God be pleased with him, to chide them and urging them to join the troops. They refused to join the troops as they did not want to fight, so they withdrew. The Messenger, peace be upon him, continued with the remaining troops, till the road to Uhud, at the bank of the valley towards the mount. He turned away from Uhud, deterring the troops from fighting till he so commanded. In the morning, he prepared his troops for fighting, among them there were fifty cavaliers and fifty shooters, presided by Abdullah ibn Jubair Alawsi, the Messenger ordered them not to move, just to protect the Muslims backlines.

Mosaab ibn Omair, brother of Banu Abduldar was given the banner. On one wing, Alzubair ibn Alawam existed, and on the other, Almonzir ibn Amr, who sought martyrdom.

Youth in troops were apparent. Those who are allowed to fight were Samura ibn Jundub and Rafie ibn Khadij, they were only fifteen

However, Osama ibn Zaid ibn Harith and Usaid ibn Zuhair, Albaraa ibn Azaib, Zaid ibn Arqam, Zaid ibn Thabet, Abdullah ibn Omar, Araba ibn Aws and Amr ibn Hazm. They were later allowed to fight in battle of the Trench (Battle of the Confederates)

Quraish was also prepared, they were three thousand; two-hundred cavilers, the right wing was taken by Khalid ibn Al-walid and the left wing was taken by Akrama ibn Abu Jahl.

From disbelievers, there was Abd Amr ibn Sefi, he had been the leader of Aws in the pre-Islamic epoch, he announced enmity towards the Messenger, peace be upon him, who asked God to take revenge from him. He left Medina and moved to Quraish urging them against the Messenger and the Muslims.

The companions of the Messenger were shouting (martyrdom, martyrdom) i.e.: they are looking for victory. Abu Dugana Simak ibn Kharsha, Hamza, the Messenger's uncle and Ali ibn Abu Talib, along with some Ansar such as Alnadr ibn Anas and Saad ibn Alrabie, all of them well did to reach victory. The disbelievers were incurred a loss and returned.

Followers of Abdullah ibn Jubair said: O' people, come and gain the booty. They thought that the disbelievers would not come back, so they rushed to gain the booty. Cavaliers of disbelievers fled, but they found an aperture free of shooters, so they exploited it, which resulted in some martyrs of believers. Some of the best companions died.

The disbelievers infiltrate to the Messenger, so he was hurt in his face and his right front teeth got broken,. His helmet was smashed. Disbelievers threw him with stones and fell in a hole made by Abu Amer to deceive the Muslims. The Messenger was then helped by Ali and hugged by Talha ibn Obaid. Amr ibn Qamiaa and Otba ibn Abu Waqas were the responsible for harming the Messenger. It is said, but it is Abdullah ibn Shihab Alzahry, the great grandfather of Muhammed ibn Muslim ibn Shihab. Mosaab ibn Omair was killed, so the banner was given to Ali ibn Abu Talib, may God be pleased with him. Two rings of the hauberk slung to the Messenger's face. Abu Obaida ibn Algarah, may God be pleased with him, removed them, and bitten them till his front teeth fell, his beauty was in his missed teeth. Malik ibn Sanan, father of Abu Said Alkhodry sucked the blood from his wound.

Disbelievers saw the Prophet, but he was protected by about ten fighters, yet they were murdered. Talha then fought them with his sword and Abu Dugana Simak ibn Kharsha shielded him by his back. Saad ibn Abu Waqas, may God be pleased with him, pointed an accurate arrow. The Messenger said: "My father and my mother are your ransom." Qatada ibn Alnoaman Althafry's eye was injured, the Messenger managed to cure him.

Satan shouted: Muhammed was killed. This hurt many Muslims.

Anas ibn Alnadr passed by the Muslims finding them discouraged, he said: what do you wait for? They replied: The

Messenger was killed. He said: what should you do after him? Hey, fight for what he fought for. He told Saad ibn Moaz: I felt the Heaven before battle of Uhud, so he fought till he was killed, seventy beats were found in his body.

Abdulrahman ibn Ouf received about twenty wounds, most of them in his leg, so he walked lamely till his death.

The Messenger, peace be upon him, directed to the Muslims, the first who knew him was Kaab Ibn Malik, may God be pleased with him. He shouted: O' Muslims, rejoice, here is the Messenger. The Messenger ordered him to keep it secret, so Muslims, including Abu Bakr, Amr, Ali and Alharith ibn Alsama Alansary gathered and directed with him towards the road he stopped at before. When they reached the mount, the Messenger was caught by Abu ibn Khalaf, when he got close, the Messenger took the bayonet from Alharith and stabbed him clavicle and fled defeated, then he died once he reached Mecca.

Ali, may God be pleased with him, brought the Messenger water to wash off the blood, but it was brackish, so he left it. The Messenger wanted to stand on a rock there, but he was too sick to go there. Talha helped him till he ascended it. It was the time of prayer, so he performed his prayer sitting. The disbelievers began to move, taking the road to Mecca.

About seventy Muslims were martyrs, among them is Hamza, uncle of the Messenger, who was killed by Wahshi, valet of Banu Nofal. For killing Hamza, he was released. After then, he converted to Islam, and killed Maslamah ibn Ḥabib. The martyrs also include Abdullah ibn Gahsh, alley of Banu Omaya, Mosaab ibn Omair, Othman ibn Othman Almakhzoumy, they four were immigrants and the rest were from Ansar.

Some elite Muslims escaped, such as Othman ibn Afan, may God be pleased with him, but God forgave them, showing this in His words: "Indeed, those of you who turned back on the day the two armies met, it was Satan who caused them to slip because of some [blame] they had earned. But God has already forgiven them. Indeed, God is Forgiving and Forbearing."" إِنَّ الَّذِينَ تَوَلَّوْا مِنكُمْ يَوْمَ الْتَقَى الْجَمْعَانِ إِنَّمَا اسْتَزَلَّهُمُ الشَّيْطَانُ بِبَعْضِ مَا كَسَبُوا وَلَقَدْ عَفَا اللَّهُ عَنْهُمْ إِنَّ اللَّهَ غَفُورٌ حَلِيمٌ" 3:155

On that day, twenty-two disbelievers were killed.

This battle was mentioned by God in Surah of Al-Imran, as He said: "And [remember] when you, [O Muhammad], left your family in the morning to post the believers at their stations for the battle [of Uhud] - and God is Hearing and Knowing"," وَإِذْ غَدَوْتَ مِنْ أَهْلِكَ تُبَوِّئُ الْمُؤْمِنِينَ مَقَاعِدَ لِلْقِتَالِ وَاللَّهُ سَمِيعٌ عَلِيمٌ" 3:121

Battle of Hamra Alasad

On Sunday, the Messenger called the Muslims to fight the enemy, and it was battle of Hamra Alasad. He ordered that only who attended battle of Uhud shall accompany him. All these who attended battle of Uhud did so, the only new was Jabir ibn Abdullah, whose father was killed in the battle of Uhud. So, he asked the Messenger to join the Muslims to Hamra Alasad, so he accepted. Muslims, despite their wounds, obeyed the Messenger, till they reached Hamra Alasad, which is eight miles from Medina. In this regard, God said: "Those [believers] who responded to God and the Messenger after injury had struck them. For those who did good among them and feared God is a great reward". " الَّذِينَ اسْتَجَابُوا لِلَّهِ وَالرَّسُولِ مِن بَعْدِ مَا أَصَابَهُمُ الْقَرْحُ لِلَّذِينَ 3:172 "أَحْسَنُوا مِنْهُمْ وَاتَّقَوْا أَجْرٌ عَظِيمٌ

Maabad ibn Abu Maabad Alkhuzaai passed by the Messenger and his companions, so he is shielded, till he reached Abu Sufian and the disbelievers in Alrawhaa, he told them that the Messenger and his companions were directing to them. This attenuated Quraish, who wanted to return to Medina, but they continued their way to Mecca.

The Messenger attained Moawia ibn Almughaira ibn Abu Alaas and ordered to be imprisoned and killed, he is father of Aisha, mother of Abd Almalek ibn Marwan.

Expedition of Alrajie

After the battle of Uhud, the Prophet, peace be upon him, continued his expeditions to Alrajie, in Safar 4 AH. So, upon their request, the Messenger sent delegates to tribes of Adal and Alqara, as they wanted to investigate Islam. He sent six individuals, according to ibn Isaac. Albukhary in his Sahih said they were ten. They were presided by Marthad ibn Abu Marthad Alghanwy, may God be pleased with him. The delegate included Khubaib ibn Oudai. At Alrajie, (a waterbody between Mecca and Aasfan), they are double-crossed and sieged by the above-mentioned tribes who killed them, but not Khubaib ibn Oudai and Zaid ibn Aldathna, who were detained. They were taken to be sold as slaves in Mecca, as a reaction to the murder of Quraish disbelievers in the battle of Badr. Khubaib stay detained, then they agreed to kill him. So, he was brought to Altaneem, a place in Mecca, to be crucified. He asked them to pray, and they accepted. He then said: I would pray more but for you would see me afraid. He then said:

I do not care for death, as I will die Muslim.

Anyway, I will return to God.

God will bless my dead body

Then they assigned a guard, Amr ibn Omaya came to carry him at night and buried him. Zaid was bought by Safwan ibn Omaya.

Abu Sufian told Zaid before being killed: Are you pleased if we kill Muhammed and you stay with your nation? He replied: I swear I am not pleased to be here with my nation and leave Muhammed endangered by any minor harm.

Expedition of Bir Maona

In the same month of Safar, a delegate was sent to Bir Maona (a will located between Banu Amer land and area of Banu Salim), as Abu Baraa Amer ibn Malik directed to the Messenger, peace be upon him, at Medina, the Messenger called him to Islam, he neither believed nor disbelieved. But he said: O' Messenger, you can send a delegate of your companions to Najd, to call its people to believe in your religion, I hope they will positively respond. The Messenger said: I am afraid Najd people would harm them. Abu Baraa said: I will protect them.

According to Isaac, the Messenger sent forty men from his companions. In both Sahihs, it was said they were seventy. The later opinion is common and true. They were presided by Almonzir ibn Amr, who belonged to Banu Saada. The delegate included the cream of Muslims, being very pious and religious. They moved to Bir Maona. From there, they sent Haram ibn Milhan, brother of Om Salim, holding the message of the Messenger to the villain, Amer ibn Altufail, who brushed away it, and ordered a man to kill Haram, and he was killed by a bayonet.

Amer called tribe of Banu Amer to fight the delegate, but they did not obey him as they were protected by Abu Baraa. But tribes of Banu Salim such as Ousia, Riel and Zakwan responded, besieging the companions of the Messenger, fighting and killing all of them, may God be pleased with them, except Kaab ibn Zaid ibn Banu Alnajar, who was injured, to be killed in the battle of the Trench.

Amr ibn Omaya Aldamry and Almounzir ibn Muhammed ibn Oqba witnessed the bird hovering around the place of the battle, so Almounzir stopped to fight the disbelievers but he was killed, and Amr ibn Omaya was detained, but Amer released him later, when he knew that he belonged to Mudhar.

Amr ibn Omaya returned, and when he was at Kana (a valley near Uhud), he rested at a shadow, with two men from Banu Kilab, they were said to be from Banu Salim. On sleep, they were killed by Amr. When he returned to the Messenger, he informed him of what he did. The Messenger replied: "You killed two, for whom I will pay blood money." This was the trigger of the battle of Banu Nadir, as mentioned in Sahih by Albukhary.

Battle of Banu Nadir

The Messenger moved to Banu Nadir to see the matter of these two victims, for the treaty between Banu Nadir and Muhammed. Banu Nadir agreed that Muhammed should be killed and called Amr ibn Gehash for this task. The messenger knew about this, so he moved, and news reached his companions, hence, they followed him. He knew about the plot of the Jews, so he called Muslims to fight them, he left Medina, assigned ibn Om Maktoum as a guardian, in Rabie al-awal, they were besieged for six nights. At that time, wine was prohibited. Only ibn Hazm stated this opinion. Abdullah ibn Abu ibn Saloul and his group of hypocrites reported to Banu Nadir: we support you, fighting with you. If you are moved, we will move with you.

They were allured by these words, so they stayed at their houses. The Messenger, peace be upon him, ordered to cut and burn their palms. So, they asked the Messenger to let them go and spar their blood in return of what their camels carry and their weapons. The Messenger so accepted. Their notability, such as Huyay ibn Akhtab and Salam ibn Abu Alhuqaiq with their households and belongings moved to Khaybar, as it is near. Others went to the Levant.

Only two of them converted to Islam; Abu Saad ibn Wahb and Yamin ibn Omair ibn Kaab, who announced a prize for who manages to kill his cousin Amr ibn Gehash, as he wanted to kill the Messenger. So, they kept their own money. The Messenger later distributed the attained money over the first immigrants and the needy Ansar Abu Dugana and Sahl ibn Hunaif. Their money was a booty, which God granted to his Messenger. In this battle, God revealed the Surah of Al-Hashr, which Abdullah ibn Abbas called Surah of Banu Nadir.

Expedition of Dhat Alriqa

The Messenger stayed a month asking God to take revenge from killers of Bir Maona. Then he launched the expedition of Dhat Alriqa, (expedition of Najd), he moved in Jumada al-awal AH, targeting Muhareb and Banu Thaaleba ibn Saad ibn Ghutfan, leaving Abu Zir Alghafary as a guardian in Medina. He walked till he found a group of Ghutfan, but no war broke out.

According to Abu Hurayrah, may God be pleased with him, the Messenger was staying in a place between Dagnan and Ousfan, besieging the disbelievers, who said: "These Muslims have a prayer that they preferred to their sons, attack them during their prayers." But Jibril came to order the messenger to divide his companions.

It is known that expedition of Ousfan was after the battle of Trench. So, expedition of Dhat Alriqa must be after Ousfan and after the battle of Khaybar. Abu Mousa Alashary and Abu Hurayrah witnessed it. Abu Mousa said that he witnessed expedition of Dhat Alriqa. Marwan ibn Alhakam asked Abu Hurayrah: Did you performed the Fear Prayer with the Messenger? He said: yes. Marwan said: when? He answered: In expedition of Najd and mentioned features of the Fear Prayer.

Some historians said that the expedition of Dhat Alriqa occurred more than once. One before the battle of the Trench and another after that of the Trench.

One of the incidents occurred in this expedition is Jabir's camel which he sold to the Messenger. Some said that this incident occurred in expedition of Tabouk. Yet, the first opinion is more suitable as his father was killed in the battle of Uhud and left seven daughters. So, Jabir had to marry a woman that can secure his sisters.

Another incident was about a man whose wife was captivated, so he swore he would kill the companions of Muhammed. So, he came at night while the Messenger had assigned two Muslim guards; Abbad ibn Bishr and Amar ibn Yasser, may God be pleased with them. So, Abbad was thrown by an arrow while he was praying. He took-out the arrow and did not stop praying till he was thrown by three arrows but in vain. Yasser told him: why did not you warn me about this man? Abbad replied: I was reciting a Surah, I preferred to complete it.

One more incident was when Ghawrath ibn Alhareth who wanted to kill the Messenger, while he was sleeping below a tree. Ghawrath unsheathed his sword and was about to lunge him, but God protected the Messenger from Ghawrath whose hand was paralyzed. The Messenger then got up and called his companions, and he told him about what Ghawrath was about to do. However, he was released and forgiven. This occurred in the expedition of Dhat Alriqa II, following the battle of the Trench.

A narration is proving this incident as Jabir ibn Abdullah said: "We were in the company of the Prophet (during the expedition of) Dhat Alriqa, and we came across a shady tree and we left it for the Prophet (to take rest under its shade). A man from the disbelievers came while the Prophet's sword was hanging on the tree. He took it out of its sheath secretly and said (to the Prophet) 'Are you afraid of me?' The Prophet said, 'No.' He said, 'Who can save you from me?' The Prophet said, God.' The companions of the Prophet threatened him, then the Iqama for the prayer was announced and the Prophet offered a two-prostration Fear prayer with one of the two batches of his companions, and that batch went aside, and he offered two prostrations with the other batch. So, the Prophet offered four prostrations, but the rest offered two only."

Minor expedition of Badr

On his departure from Uhud, Abu Sufian shouted: we will meet next year in Badr, the Messenger, peace be upon him ordered some of his companions to say "yes". In Shaaban of that year, the Messenger went to Badr on time and left Abdulah ibn Abu as a guardian in Medina, he stayed there for eight nights and then returned with no war, as Abu Sufian moved with some troops of Quraish, and on their way they had to return because they suffered a barren year. This incident was named the promised Badr.

Expedition of Dumat Aljandal

The Messenger went to Dumat Aljandal in Rabie al-awal 5 AH, then he returned as the war did not break out. At that time, he was leaving Medina under the guardianship of Sibaa ibn Orfuta.

Battle of the Trench

It is the battle when God examined his servants and fixed faith in the hearts of his best. It is when God showed up the hypocrites, supported the Muslims and defeated confederates, cherished his soldiers, riposted the disbelievers and protected the believers from their evils.

The battle occurred in Shawal 5 AH, this cannot be disputed because the battle of Uhud was in Shawal 3 AH, and Abu Sufian was intending to meet the Muslims in the minor battle of Badr after a year from Uhud, but Quraish withdrew because of their barren year.

Abu Muhammed ibn Hazm Alandalusy in his book "Almaghazi" refuted that and claimed that the true date is in 4 AH, this opinion is also adopted by Mousa ibn Oqba. Ibn Hazm argues, based on the narration by ibn Omar: "The Messenger of God inspected me on the battlefield on the Day of Uhud, and I was fourteen years old. He did not allow me (to take part in the fight). He inspected me on the day of the battle of the Trench, and I was fifteen years old, and he permitted me (to fight)".

The battle of the Trench was triggered because some Jews of Banu Nadir who were deported by the Messenger to Khaybar, they were their notability (Salam ibn Abu Alhuqaiq, Salam ibn Mishkam, Kinanah ibn Alrabie and others) went to Quraish in Mecca, to urge them to fight the Messenger, Quraish accepted. Then they directed to Ghutfan, who positively responded. Thus, Quraish presided by Abu Sufian ibn Harb and Ali Ghutfan Ayayna ibn Hesn, accompanied by about ten thousand fighters moved out. When the Messenger knew about their patrol, he ordered the Muslims to dig a trench to hinder the disbelievers from entering Medina. This was pointed by Salman Alfarsy, so the Muslims started digging. While digging of the trench, many sings of Muhammed's prophecy appeared. When it is complete, the disbelievers arrived, to stop around Medina, as God said: "[Remember] when they came at you from above you and from below you". 33:10 "إِذْ جَاءُوكُم مِّن فَوْقِكُمْ وَمِنْ أَسْفَلَ مِنكُمْ"

The Messenger and his three thousand fighters were fortified by the trench, turned their back to Mount Sela. The Messenger ordered that women and children must stay home in Medina that was left under the guardianship of ibn Om Maktoum, may God be pleased with him.

Huyay ibn Akhtab moved to Banu Qurayza to meet their leader Kaab ibn Saad. He urged Kaab to breach the treaty between Qurayza and the Messenger. Kaab so accepted and agreed to fight the Messenger, that pleased the disbelievers.

The Messenger sent Saad ibn Moaz, Saad ibn Obada, Khawat ibn Jubair and Abdullah ibn Rawaha, to make sure whether Banu Qurayza breached the treaty. When reached there, they found Banu Qurayza announcing enmity and treachery. So, they began to insult one another, the Jews, may God curse them, insulted the Messenger. Thus, Jews were insulted by Saad ibn Moaz and left. The Messenger ordered them previously that if Banu Qurayza breached the treaty, this must not be reported to the Muslims, lest they should lose their power. Only they can secretly report this to the Messenger if happened. He said: who is following you? They said: Adal and Alqara, implying to their treachery towards martyrdoms of Alrajie. Thus, the danger became greater. God said in this context: "There the believers were tested and shaken with a severe shaking."'' هُنَالِكَ ابْتُلِيَ الْمُؤْمِنُونَ 11:33"وَزُلْزِلُوا زِلْزَالًا شَدِيدًا

Hypocrisy was shown up, and some of Banu Haritha asked the Messenger, peace be upon him, to leave to Medina for their families.

Disbelievers stayed a month besieging the Messenger, with no war, as the trench was protecting the Messenger, peace be upon him, and his troops. However, some of Quraish cavaliers such as Amr ibn Abd Wad Alamry and others directed to the trench and astonished saying: this is an artifice not known previously by the Arabs, then they betook themselves to a narrow place in the trench, breaking through and passing. Their horses were cruising between the bog between the trench and Mount Sela, calling for fight. So, Amr ibn Abd Wad called Ali ibn Abu Talib, may God be pleased with him, for fight, Ali managed to kill Amr who was over a hundred years at that time, whose courage was unprecedented in the pre-Islamic epoch. The rest of them fled returning to their home. Muslims were shouting: "Ha-Mim, they will not be victorious"

When this lasted long, the Messenger wanted to conclude a reconciliation with Ayayna ibn Hesn and Alharith ibn Ouf, leaders of Ghutfan for one third of the crops of Medina, to deport with their troops. The Messenger consulted both Saad ibn Moaz and Saad ibn Obada. They said: O' Messenger, if God ordered you to do so, we will obey. If you are doing so for us, so we and they were polytheists, and they could not eat a fruit from Medina but out of hospitality or sale. So, when we are honored by Islam and you, shall we give them our money?! They only deserve to be killed. He replied: "I just want to do so for your benefit". Then he expressed his willingness towards their opinions and did not conclude the reconciliation.

Subsequently, God granted victory to the Muslims and defeated the disbelievers, as Nuaim ibn Masoud ibn Amer Alghutfany, may God be pleased with him, came to the Messenger saying: I converted to Islam, so you can order me to do whatever you want. The Messengerm peace be upon him, replied: "But you are alone, urge them to leave the battlefield, if you can, the war is a play". So, he went to Banu Qurayza, as he was a friend of them before Islam, they were not informed of his conversion to Islam. He told them: Banu Qurayza, you fought Muhammed, and Quraish could take the opportunity if any, but they returned, and left you but Muhammed will revenge. They said: so, what could we do, Nuaim? He said: Do not fight them. They replied: So, this is your opinion.

Then he moved to Quraish and told Abu Sufian and his tribe: Do you know that I wish you the best? They said: yes. He said: the Jews regretted their breach of their treaty with Muhammed and the Muslims and told him that they would take some hostages from you to him, then they will support him against you. Thereafter, he directed to his nation, Ghutfan, saying the same.

On Saturday night in Shawal, Quraish sent a message to the Jews: we must go tomorrow to fight this man. The Jews replied: it is Saturday, we will not fight, until you send us hostages. So, Quraish believed Nuaim ibn Masoud. Quraish told the Jews: we will not send hostages, move with us to the battle. So, Qurayza believed Nuaim, and refused to join Quraish in fighting.

So, the Messenger sent to Quraish winds blew their tents, so they were weakened. He then sent Huthaifa ibn Alyaman to trace their conditions, so he found them in a miserable condition. Huthaifa saw Abu Sufian sitting close to a fire for warmness, Huthaifa could kill him. Yet, he returned to the Messenger at night, informing him of their departure.

When the Messenger returned in the morning to Medina, as people were disarmed, Jibril came to the Messenger, when he was resting at Om Salma's home, saying: are you disarmed? For us, we are not. Banu Qurayza will be demolished.

Siege of Banu Qurayza

The Messenger moved to Banu Qurayza, ordering the Muslims not to perform the Afternoon Prayer – although it is time for it – but at Banu Qurayza. So, the Muslims obeyed, from them are some who performed the prayer on road. It is said that the Messenger did not want to leave the prayer, but he wanted us to move quickly. There are some who did not perform the prayer till it was sunset and reached Banu Qurayza. But the Messenger did not blame any of them.

Ibn Hazm said: these are right and those are mistaken but rewarded. If we were there, we would not perform the Afternoon Prayer but in Banu Qurayza, even if after several days.

Some opinions said in this regard, that neither was mistaken, but a batch would be rewarded twice, and another would be rewarded once.

It is said that the last Afternoon and Sunset Prayers were on the day of the battle of the Trench, so some were keen on prayer, God said: "Maintain with care the [obligatory] prayers and [in particular] the middle prayer and stand before God, devoutly obedient." "حَافِظُوا عَلَى الصَّلَوَاتِ وَالصَّلَاةِ الْوُسْطَىٰ وَقُومُوا لِلَّهِ قَانِتِينَ " **2:238**

On the battle day of the Trench, the Messenger said: "'(Let) God fill their (i.e. the infidels') houses and graves with fire just as they have prevented us from offering the Middle Prayer (i.e. Afternoon Prayer) till the sun had set."

To conclude this matter, who performed the Afternoon Prayer on the road, understood what was implicitly intended by the Messenger and were rewarded twice. The others obeyed his express order, so they were rewarded once.

The Messenger gave the flag to Ali ibn Abu Talib and assigned ibn Om Maktoum as a guardian in Medina. He then went to forts of Banu Qurayza and besieged them for twenty-five nights.

Their leader Kaab ibn Asad offered them three options: either to convert to Islam, to kill their own children and be disarmed then fight till God judge between them or to attack the Messenger and his troops on Saturday as they will not expect the fight. Huyay ibn Akhtab joined them in their forts. The Messenger would like to talk to them, but Ali advised him not to go as if he did, he would be harmed.

He sent Abu Lubaba ibn Abd Almonzir Alawsy, as Aws and Qurayza were allies. They asked him about his opinion, he referred to slaughter of Muhammad. He then regretted this word and hurled to the Medina mosque attaching himself to a pillar there; vowing that he would not release himself, till the Messenger so did and he would not never go to Banu Qurayza. The Messenger, peace be upon him, arrived and ordered people to leave him saying: "let him go so God would forgive him".

Thaalba ibn Saia, Usid ibn Saia and Asad ibn Obaid, who belonged to Banu Hadl, cousins of Qurayza and Nadir. Amr ibn Sudi Alqarzy fled and nobody knew his place, he was rejecting breach of the treaty.

Aws said: O' Messenger, you let Abdullah ibn Abu interceded for Banu Qaynuqa, who are allies of Khazraj, our associates. He said: Would not you like them to be ruled by a man from you? They said: Yes. He said: He would be Saad ibn Moaz. Saad at that time was injured in his ankle. The Messenger made him a tent in the mosque. Then he was called by the Messenger and was brought while his brothers from Aws surrounding him, saying: O' Abu Amr, be kind with your allies. When they repeated their words. He replied: It is time for me not to fear blame of blamers. When the Messenger came to Banu Qurayza, he said: "Stand for your master". So, Muslims stood, saying: "O' Saad, the Messenger appointed you to judge Banu Qurayza." He resolved that the Jewish killers would be killed, children would be captured, and their money should be taken and distributed over the Muslims; a share for the infantry soldier and three for the cavalier. On that day, the Muslims had thirty-six cavaliers.

Saad asked God saying: If war against Quraish will continue, let me alive. If it is done, I prefer to die. But do not claim my life, unless I took revenge from Banu Qurayza. The Messenger cauterized his wound, but it burst and died.

Sending Abdullah ibn Atik to kill Abu Rafie Salam ibn Abu Alhuqaiq

When Kaab ibn Alashraf was killed by men from Aws after the battle of Badr. Abu Rafie is that who urged the confederates to fight the Messenger, he was not killed in Banu Qurayza as his friend Huyay ibn Akhtab. Khazraj wanted to kill him to be equal with Aws. So, they asked the Messenger of God to kill him, he accepted, so, men were called, all of them were from Banu Salma; Abdullah ibn Atik, the leader of his nation, Abdullah ibn Anis, Abu Qatada Alharith ibn Rubie, Masoud ibn Sanan and Khuzaie ibn Aswad, an alley of them. They moved to him, catching him in Khaybar. He was killed at night and returned to the Messenger. All claimed killing him. The Messenger said: "show me your swords". The Messenger said the killer is Abdullah ibn Anis, who instilled his sword in his body till bones of his back was heard cracking. The enemy was screaming: "my back".

Expedition of Banu Lahyan

Six months after Qurayza, in Jumada al-awal 6 AH, the Messenger went to Banu Lahyan to take revenge for martyrs of Alrajie. He walked to Ghuran valley, between Amag and Ousfan, he found them fortified in the mountain tops, so he left with two-hundred cavaliers till he stopped at Ousfan and sent two to Keraa Alghamim (a place between Mecca and Medina), they retreated and returned to Medina

Expedition of Dhu Qarad

Several days after, Ayayna ibn Hesn appeared accompanied by Banu Abdullah ibn Ghutfan, riding the camel of the Messenger that was in the forest, after killing the herdsman, a man in Ghifar, and took his wife. Salma ibn Amr ibn Alakwaa Alaslamy, may God be pleased with him, was in his guard against them, then he hurtled, walking and he cannot be outrun, he began darting them.

When shouting was heard in Medina, the Messenger moved with some cavaliers, following Salma ibn Alakwaa and attain back the camel. The Prophet reached a waterbody called Qarad, he stayed there a day and a night, then returned to Medina.

In this expedition, Alakhram, Mahraz ibn Nadla was killed by Abdulrahman ibn Ayayna and rode his horse. Horses were attained by Mahmoud ibn Maslama. The captivated woman returned on the Messenger's camel. She vowed if she is rescued, she will slaughter the camel. The Messenger said: "There is no vow for the son of Adam with regard to that which he does not possess, or to do an act of disobedience to God", he retained his camel. In his Sahih, Imam Muslim narrated this story, quoting Salma ibn Alaqwaa, saying: then we returned to Medina, to stay there only three nights, then went to Khaybar.

Expedition of Banu Mustaliq

The Messenger, peace be upon him, moved to Khuzaa of Banu Mustaliq, in Saaban 6 AH, it was said that the expedition was in Saaban 5 AH. Yet the first opinion is more common, adopted by ibn Isaac and others.

The Messenger left Abu Zir as a guardian for Medina, some said but Numaila ibn Abdullah Alaithy, they were attacked inattentively, at a will called Muraysi, near Qadid, between Mecca and Medina. Some were killed there. Muslims at that day were shouting: "We seek martyrdom".

From female captives is Juayraia, daughter of Alharith ibn Abu Drar, leader of Banu Mustaliq, gained by Thabet ibn Qais ibn Shamas. The Messenger paid her blood money, and got married to her, then she became a Mother of Believers (Om

Almoemenin). As a result, a hundred families from Banu Mustaliq were released.

Abdullah ibn Abu ibn Saloul was denouncing at that time the existence of the Muslims in Medina, claiming that the prestigious were moved out, and slurring the Messenger. Zaid ibn Arqam was informed of Abdullah's words. He so reported to the Messenger, who doubted the truth of such news, till God showed the credibility of Zaid in Surah of Al-Monafuqoun (the hypocrites).

From incidents of this expedition was the falsehood by Abdullah ibn Abu Saloul and his group of hypocrites. Aisha, daughter of Abu Bakr, may God be pleased with her, moved out with the Messenger in this expedition, and she was carried in a squaw. In the morning, they wanted to depart, she went to the toilet, and on her return, she found that she lost her necklace, originally belonged to her sister Asmaa. She returned to the toilet to look for it, while people who were carrying her squaw took it to leave, not stunned by its lightweight, as she already was tiny of fourteen years old. When she returned, after she found her necklace, she did not find the squaw. She waited guessing that they would miss her and return. She had a nap and only got up when Safwan ibn Almuatal Alsulmy and Alzakwany saying: "Indeed we belong to God and indeed to Him we will return", they were there to take a break from travelling. When Safwan witnessed her, he said: "Indeed we belong to God and indeed to Him we will return". He gave her his camel to ride it, while he did not utter a word to her. Yet she was not left by Abu

Saloul and his group of hypocrites who started to slur her and create a falsehood about her. Yet, God words denounced their action: "Indeed, those who came with falsehood are a group among you. Do not think it is bad for you; rather it is good for you". " إِنَّ الَّذِينَ جَاءُوا بِالْإِفْكِ عُصْبَةٌ مِّنكُمْ ۚ لَا تَحْسَبُوهُ شَرًّا لَّكُم ۖ بَلْ هُوَ خَيْرٌ لَّكُمْ ۚ". "لِكُلِّ امْرِئٍ مِّنْهُم مَّا اكْتَسَبَ مِنَ الْإِثْمِ ۚ وَالَّذِي تَوَلَّىٰ كِبْرَهُ مِنْهُمْ لَهُ عَذَابٌ عَظِيمٌ". **24:11**

After God revealed these verses one month after returning from the expedition, those who talked about the falsehood were laced, such as Mistah ibn Athatha and Hamna bint Gahsh.

The Messenger, peace be upon him, was on the pulpit and ask the Muslims to grant victory over Abdullah ibn Abu Saloul and his group, saying: who could grant me victory over a man harmed me with my family? I know all the best about my family and the man whom they falsely accused, who always was with me when he entered my house" Saad ibn Moaz, brother of Banu Abd Alashhal said: O' Messenger, I could do this and grant you victory over him. If he is from Aws, I will kill him, if he is from Khazraj, we will obey your order. Saad ibn Obada said: you cannot kill him, if he was one from your family, you would not prefer him to be killed. Asid ibn Alhudair: I swear I will kill him, he is a hypocrite talking with a group of hypocrites. The discussion flamed till they were about to fight each other. Yet the Messenger started to calm them down.

However, it is doubted as Saad ibn Moaz died after Qurayza which was after the battle of the Trench, in 5 AH. The falsehood happened in expedition of Banu Mustaliq.

Imam Muhammed ibn Isaac said that the expedition of Banu Mustaliq was in 6 AH, when falsehood happened but he cited the narration, not mentioning Saad ibn Moaz, as Asid ibn Alhudair said: I will grant you victory over him.

Treaty of Hudaybiyyah

In Zulqida (the eleventh month of the Islamic calendar), 6 AH, moved to perform Umrah with a thousand and some people. They were said to be five-hundred, four-hundred and three-hundred.

When the disbelievers knew about that, they gathered their allies, to keep him off Umrah this year, sending Khalid ibn Al-walid to Keraa Alghamim. The Messenger failed to meet him on the way, but he reached Hudaybiyyah, exchanging messages with the disbelievers, till Suhail ibn Amr came to make peace with him for his return to Medina and postponing the Umrah for the following year. The Messenger, peace be upon him, so accepted yet some of the companions so abhorred; such as Omar ibn Alkhatab. So, Suhail ibn Amr agreed with him that the Messenger would return to Medina and would come in the following year to perform his Umrah, provided that he would not enter Mecca, but with his sword sheathed and he would not stay there more than three days. They also agreed to let whoever wanted to convert to Islam and whoever wanted to continue being on Quraysh's religion. They agreed that if a person belonged to Quraysh came to the Messenger, even if he was Muslim, he would repudiate him, and if a Muslim came to them, he will not be repudiated. Yet, this provision was later controverted by Quraish as the repudiated Muslims were representing a peril to Quraysh.

God so adopted, yet for the last provision, it would not apply on the female immigrants, as they would not be repudiated to the disbelievers, as they were prohibited to marry a disbeliever.

Before the treaty, the Messenger, peace be upon him, sent Othman ibn Afan, may God be pleased with him, to Mecca people, informing them he would not be there for a war but for Umrah. Being one of the special nobilities, he was offered circumambulation, but he refused to do so without the Messenger.

Thereafter he did not return to the Messenger, he was killed, so the Messenger was flared up, and called his companions to pledge allegiance to him for fighting. They so did at a tree and joined him to Hudaybiyya, except ibn Qais. Abu Sariha Huthaifa ibn Asid attended the treaty of Hudaybiyya, it is controverted whether he pledged allegiance to the Messenger or not.

Who pledged allegiance to the Messenger are Abu Sinan Wahb ibn Mihsan, brother of Ukasha ibn Mihsan, and Sinan ibn Abu Sinan. Salma ibn Alakwaa also pledged allegiance to the Messenger three times, as he put one hand on the Messenger saying: that for Othman. In this regard, God said: "Certainly was God pleased with the believers when they pledged allegiance to you, [O Muhammad], under the tree, and He knew what was in their hearts, so He sent down tranquility upon them and reward-ed them with an imminent conquest" " لَّقَدْ رَضِيَ اللَّهُ عَنِ الْمُؤْمِنِينَ إِذْ يُبَايِعُونَكَ تَحْتَ الشَّجَرَةِ فَعَلِمَ مَا فِي قُلُوبِهِمْ فَأَنزَلَ السَّكِينَةَ عَلَيْهِمْ وَأَثَابَهُمْ فَتْحًا قَرِيبًا"48:18

This is called Pledge of the Tree, Pledge of Ridwan (Pledge of Satisfaction).

Some were upset with this, as they wanted to perform their Umrah, they found the disbelievers forcing them to do what they want after approval by the Messenger. Yet this approval is a great bravery. When he was returning to Medina, God revealed Surah of Al-Fateh as a whole, in this regard. Abdullah ibn Ma-soud said: you consider this conquest of Mecca, yet we consider it of Hudaybiyya, this is deeply true. This conquest is the ground for the conquest of Mecca 8 AH, as mentioned later.

Battle of Khaybar

When the Messenger returned to Medina, he stayed there till Almuharam (the first month of the Islamic calendar) 7 AH, at the end of it, he moved to Khaybar. Date of this battle is controverted, yet the common is that the battle occurred in 7 AH. The Messenger went to Khaybar, leaving Numaila ibn Abdullah Alaithy, and when arrived, he besieged its forts, distributing its half over the Muslims, all of them were those who attended the Treaty of Hudaybiyya, the other half was assigned to his benefit and the Muslims matters. Safeya, daughter of Huyay ibn Akhtab converted to Islam and so he married her.

A Jewish female, Zainab, daughter of Alharith and wife of Salam ibn Mishkam, offered the Messenger a serous poisoned sheep, when the Messenger took its arm, he was told by it that it is poisoned, so he did not eat, then called the Jewish female asking her: "Did you intoxicate this sheep? She said: yes, He asked: Why? She answered: I wanted to check if you are a prophet, this sheep will not harm you, if not, we will get rid of you. So, he forgave her. However, it was said that Bishr ibn Albara ibn Marour ate of it, he died, so she killed. This was said by Abu Dawoud, according to Abu Salma ibn Abdulrahman ibn Ouf.

At the time of the battle, after they are done with fighting against the enemies, Gaefer ibn Abu Talib, his companions who still in Ethiopia, Abu Mousa Alashary, some of his tribe more than seventy and Abu Hurayrah visited the Messenger, so he gave them some of the booty. He said to Gaefer: I do not know by which shall I be pleased: our victory in Khaybar or Gaefer's arrival? He kissed his forehead.

About twenty Muslims were martyred, at the battle of Khaybar.

Conquest of Fadak

When people of Fadak (tract of land) knew what the Messenger, peace be upon him, did with Khaybar people, he sent to him asking for treaty, Muslims did enter it as cavaliers and the Messenger did not divide it.

Conquest of Wadi Alqara

He returned to Wadi Alqara (a valley between Tayma and Khaybar). It is said that the Messenger fought there. In both books of Sahih, a valet of the Messenger called Midam, while preparing the Messenger belongings, was thrown by an arrow that claimed his life, people said: he won martyrdom. The Messenger said: the mantle Midam was granted from the booty will not be regranted to anyone, it will be burnt for him

Umrah of Alqadaa

When the Messenger returned to Medina, he stayed till Zulqida, he then directed to perform Umrah of Alqadaa, it is compensating the missed Umrah of the previous year. Some said that it is Umrah of revenge. All opinions are common and true.

He reached Mecca and performed his Umrah circumambulating. After completing his Umrah, he married Maymouna, daughter of Alharith. Three days later, the disbelievers told him: leave our land, he replied: what would you say if I married Maymouna here? They refused. At that time, they left Mecca when he came, out of enmity and hatred.

Battle of Muta

In Jumada al-akher, 8 AH, the Messenger, peace be upon him, sent leaders to Muta (a village in the Levant), to take revenge from Muslims killed there. He assigned Zaid Ibn Haritha to rule, saying: "If Zaid is injured, Gaefer Ibn Abu Talib will rule, and if injured, Abdullah Ibn Rawaha will rule"

They went accompanied by three-thousand fighters, and the Messenger to farewell them. They moved till Maan, as they were informed that Hercules, king of Rome was directing to them, with a hundred-thousand fighters and Malik Ibn Zafila, with a hundred-thousand fighters of Christian Arabs from Lakhm and Guzam, as well as tribes of Bahraa and Bali from Qudaa. So, the Muslims consulted each other; saying: we have to message the Messenger to advise us or provide us with more troops. Abdullah Ibn Rawaha said: O' people, you moved to seek martyrdom and you are fighting not supported by power or troops but supported by this religion. So, we are seeking either victory or martyrdom.

When they reached Balqaa margins, they found the Romans, so they stopped by Muta and the Romans in a village called Masharif, and then they fought each other.

Muslims leader, Zaid ibn Haritha was killed, holding the flag, which was given later to Gaefer, who fought till his right hand was cut then he took the flag with the left hand, which was then also cut, so he hugged the flag, but eventually he was killed, when he was thirty-three. Abdullah ibn Rawaha took the flag, may God be pleased with him. He waited but then fought till his life was claimed. It is said that Thabet ibn Akram took the flag and the Muslims wanted to appoint him as a leader, yet he so refused. Khalid ibn Alwalid took the flag and supported the Muslims till they got rid of the enemy. The corpses of the three martyred leaders were brought to the Messenger, while he was shedding tears over them.

Although the enemy existed in huge troops, unlike the Muslims, only about ten Muslims were killed.

Muslims returned, yet this battle was the trigger of the later Muslim-Roman battles, that terrorized the enemies.

Conquest of Mecca

Khuzaa joined the Messenger side in the treaty of Hudaybiyya and Banu Bakr joined Quraish, the treaty was concluded for ten years, from which only a year and nine months passed. Yet, Aldeli tribe presided by Nofal and some of Banu Bakr ibn Abd Monat fought with Khuzaa. Quraish supported Banu Bakr, arming them to fight Khuzaa that fled to Kaaba and traced by Banu Bakr.

Some people from Khuzaa such as Amr ibn Salim Alkhuzaay and Budail ibn Warqaa Alkhuzaay came to the Messenger, peace be upon him, informing him of what Quraish did and asking him for support. Abu Sufian then came to the Messenger to renew the treaty, but the Messenger refused, after consulting Abu Bakr, Omar ibn Alkhatab, and Ali ibn Abu Talib, who all rejected renewal, declaring war against them.

Then the Messenger began moving to Mecca, asking God that Quraish would not know about such movement. God responded. Hatib Ibn Abu Baltaa sent a message with a woman to Mecca, informing them of the Messenger's intentions. Ali, Alzubair and Almiqdad were sent to drive this woman back and take the message from her. This was a sign of the Messenger's prophecy.

He moved on 10th Ramadan, with ten-thousand fighters from immigrants, Ansar and Arab tribes, leaving Medina under the guardianship of Abu Ruhm Kaltoum ibn Hasin. He met his uncle Alabbas in Zulhulaifa, near Medina, others said: in Aljahfa, who converted to Islam and sent his family to Medina.

When the Messenger, peace be upon him reached Nik Aloqab (a place between Mecca and Medina), his cousin Abu Sufian ibn Alharith ibn Abdulmutlib and Abdullah Ibn Abu Omaya, brother of Om Salma as Muslims, but he dismissed them, yet Om Salma interceded, so he welcomed them, and they converted to Islam after they were the fiercest with him.

The Messenger was fasting till he reached a will called Alkudaid, between Ousfan and Amag, but he broke his fast at the afternoon, so people could see him and allow them to break their fast.

For Quraish, it did not know this news. At that night, Sufian ibn Harb, Budail Ibn Warqaa and Hakim ibn Hazam went to get information about their conditions. When they saw flames, they wondered thereabout. Budail said: it is Khuzaa's flames, yet Abu Sufian said: Khuzaa is not strong enough to do this.

Earlier, Alabbas was moving to find anyone from the disbelievers and found Abu Sufian, he managed to bring him on his camel. Then, the troops passed by people and when they saw Alabbas among them, they said: this is the Messenger's uncle riding the Messenger's camel, till he arrived at house of Omar ibn Alkhatab, when he saw Abu Sufian, said: the enemy of God? Thanks to God that I found you with no pact or treaty.

Both were running, but Omar was slow, so he was out run by Alabbas, and he brought Abu Sufian to the Messenger, peace be upon him, and was followed by Omar. Alabbas asked the Messenger to kill Abu Sufian, but he refused and talked to Abu Sufian, offering him to embrace Islam. He hesitated, but then he embraced Islam.

Alabbas said: O' Messenger. Abu Sufian is a man who likes taking the pride, if you may do something for him. He said: "Yes, he who enters the house of Abu Sufian is safe, and he who closes his door is safe. And who enters Alharam mosque is safe."

Ibn Hazm said: this is a clear evidence that Islam spread in Mecca by conciliation not force. Another evidence is that Mecca was not divided. Some said but there were some people killed from Quraish at Mount Alkhandama.

The Messenger went to the house of Om Hanie, daughter of Abu Talib, the Messenger's uncle, in Mecca, to wash and pray there eight prostrations. Some said it is the Forenoon Prayer, others said: it is a prayer to thank God for the victory. Then he directed to the Kaaba circumambulating only.

He took the key of the Kaaba and entered it removing idols therefrom. On that day, Bilal called for prayer on the Kaaba, then the Messenger returned the key to Othman ibn Talha ibn Abu Talha. The conquest occurred on 20th Ramadan.

The Messenger then sent expeditions to Arabs around Mecca, calling them for Islam, such as sending Khalid ibn Alwalid to Banu Gazima who were killed by Khalid as they did not convert to Islam, yet the Messenger paid their blood money and denounced Khalid's act.

Khalid was sent to Aloza (one of the three chief goddesses worshiped by the pre-Islamic Arabs), whom Quraish, Kinanah and all who belonged to Mudhr respected, yet he managed to demolish the same.

Akrama ibn Abu Jahl fled to Yemen, followed by his Muslim wife, Om Hakim bint Alharith ibn Hisham, she got him back as the Messenger will secure him. So, he converted to Islam.

Safwan ibn Omaya also fled to Yemen, followed by his friend Amir ibn Wahb offering him to be safe with the Messenger, he got Safwan back, and converted to Islam.

Battle of Hunayn

When Banu Hawazin was informed of conquest of Mecca and prevailing of Islam there, Malik ibn Ouf Alnasry gathered them, along with Banu Thaqif, Banu Nasr ibn Moawya, Banu Gushm, Banu Saad ibn Bakr, Banu Bishr ibn Hilal ibn Amer. They moved taking with them, their cattle and wives so that they could not flee. When Duraid ibn Alsama, leader of Banu Gushm (who was carried in a squaw being old, but for his opinion) knew that, he denounced act of Malik, saying: this would not help. He urged them that they should only fight in their land, but they refused, obeying Malik.

The Messenger, peace be upon him, sent Abdullah Ibn Abu Hadrad Alaslamy, to inspect their intentions, so the Messenger stand prepared to meet them and borrowed from Safwan ibn Omaya a hundred (some said four hundred) armors and some money and moved to the enemy with ten-thousand fighters who previously joined the Messenger in the conquest of Mecca and two-thousand others who were converted to Islam on the conquest of Mecca. Safwan ibn Omaya attended the day of Hunayn, despite being a disbeliever, in Shawal, the Messenger left Mecca under the guardianship of Asid ibn Abu Aleis ibn Omaya ibn Abd Shama, when he was about twenty. On his way, he passed by a tree worshipped by the disbelievers called Zat Anwat; so, some ignorant Arabs said: O Messenger! Make us a Zat Anwat as they have a Zat Anwat. The Prophet said: Glory be to God! This is like what Musa's people said: Make for us a god like their gods. By the One in Whose hand is my soul! You shall follow the way of those who were before you.

Then he reached Hunayn (a valley belongs to Tuhama valleys), where Hawazin settled. At dawn, they attacked the Muslims, who started to flee. God said: "And [even] on the day of Hunayn, when your great number pleased you, but it did not avail you at all, and the earth was confining for you with its vastness; then you turned back, fleeing." " وَيَوْمَ حُنَيْنٍ ۙ إِذْ أَعْجَبَتْكُمْ "كَثْرَتُكُمْ فَلَمْ تُغْنِ عَنكُمْ شَيْئًا وَضَاقَتْ عَلَيْكُمُ الْأَرْضُ بِمَا رَحُبَتْ ثُمَّ وَلَّيْتُم مُّدْبِرِينَ 9:25

Some of them said: we will gain victory in spite of our small number, the Messenger and the companions: Abu Bakr, Omar, Ali, Alabbas, Alfadl, Qutham, Abu Sufian ibn Alharith ibn Abdulmutlib and his son Gaefer did not flee. The Messenger was riding his camel, that he was given by Farwa ibn Nufatha Alguzamy, directing towards the enemy, Alabbas grabbed its bridle to stop it. The Messenger was saying:

"I am the Prophet, I do not lie, I am the son of Abdulmutlib"

Alabbas, with his deep loud voice, called: O' Ansar, O' pledge attenders. So, when Muslim heard him after fleeing, they shouted: Here we are at your service. If the cavalier could not move with his horse because of the big number of the defeated, he would leave his horse and took his armor and sword and ran to the Messenger, until they formed a hundred-fighter troop, they fought with Hawazin and the war got worse. Hawazin became frightened and the Messenger throw a fistful of pebbles, as God said: " And you threw not, [O Muhammad], when you threw, but it was God who threw" " فَلَمْ تَقْتُلُوهُمْ وَلَٰكِنَّ اللَّهَ قَتَلَهُمْ ۚ وَمَا رَمَيْتَ إِذْ رَمَيْتَ وَلَٰكِنَّ اللَّهَ رَمَىٰ ۚ وَلِيُبْلِيَ الْمُؤْمِنِينَ مِنْهُ بَلَاءً حَسَنًا ۚ إِنَّ اللَّهَ سَمِيعٌ عَلِيمٌ" 8:17

Hawazin fled from the Muslims who followed them to kill and seize its fighters, as each companion was brining to the Messenger captives.

Some of Hawazin aligned themselves to Awtas, so the Messenger sent Obaid Abu Amer Alashary, his nephew Abu Mousa Alashary, the flag holder, along with some Muslims. Abu Amer was killed, as a man shot his knee. So, Abu Mousa killed the killer. Some said, the killer was not killed but he later converted to Islam.

Abu Amer was the forth martyr of Hunayn. The other three were Ayman ibn Om Ayman, Yaziz ibn Zamaa ibn Alaswad and Suraqa ibn Alharith ibn Oudai from Banu Uglan from Ansar.

For the disbelievers, about forty were killed.

In this battle, the Messenger said: "Whoever kills someone in battle, having a proof for that, then his goods are his."

Siege of Taif

For king of Hawazin, Malik ibn Ouf Alnasri, when his army was defeated, he joined Thaqif in Taif fort. The Messenger returned from Hunayn, he did not enter Mecca till he reached Taif to siege its people. The siege lasted for twenty and some nights, according to some opinions, others said but for a ten and some nights. The first opinion is supported by the Messenger's words: "I waited for you twenty nights". In Sahih, Anas ibn Malik said: we sieged them for forty days, and they killed some Muslims.

The Messenger gained a lot of their money and demolished their plants, he did not attain a lot from them, so he left going to Aljurana, a will between Mecca and Taif. There some of Hawazin came as Muslims, before booties distribution. He let them choose either their children or money, they chose the children. He said: "As for that which was allocated to me and to Banu Abdulmutlib, it is yours." The immigrants said: 'That which was allocated to us is for the Messenger.' The Ansar said: 'That which was allocated to us is for the Messenger.' Alaqra ibn Habis said: 'As for me and Banu Tamim, then no (we will not give it up).' Ayayna ibn Hisn said: 'As for me and Banu Fazarah, then no (we will not give it up).' Alabbas ibn Mirdas said: 'As for me and Banu Sulaim, then no (we will not give it up).' Banu Sulaim stood up and said: 'You lied; whatever was allocated to us, it is for the Messenger. Hawazin then regained their children, who were six thousand, of them is Alshaimaa, daughter of Alharith ibn Abd Aloza, from Banu Saad ibn Bakr ibn Hawazin, the foster-sister of the Messenger, so he treated her generously and returned willingly to her land. It was said that Hawazin is affiliated to the Messenger as they feed him as an infant.

The rest was distributed over the Muslims. According to Alzahry, the Messenger gave Safwan ibn Omaya three-hundred camels.

Ansar blamed him for that, he then met them and treated them generously, so they were satisfied.

Harqous Zul Khwaisara Altamimy defamed the Prophet regarding the booty distribution but he was forgiven. Some Muslim leaders said: Should I not strike his neck? Upon this the Messenger said: No. A people would rise from his progeny who would recite Qur'an, if you find them, certainly kill them."

He assigned Malik as a leader for those people who converted to Islam, who was also himself converted to Islam, he later praised the Messenger in a poem.

The Messenger entered Mecca to perform Umrah and when he so completed, he directed to Medina. Asid also leaded people to perform Umrah, so he was the first Muslims leader to do so.

Expedition of Tabouk

When God revealed his verses to The Messenger; "Fight those who do not believe in God or in the Last Day and who do not consider unlawful what God and His Messenger have made unlawful and who do not adopt the religion of truth from those who were given the Scripture - [fight] until they give the jizyah willingly while they are humbled.". " قَاتِلُوا الَّذِينَ لَا يُؤْمِنُونَ بِاللَّهِ وَلَا بِالْيَوْمِ الْآخِرِ وَلَا يُحَرِّمُونَ مَا حَرَّمَ اللَّهُ وَرَسُولُهُ وَلَا يَدِينُونَ دِينَ الْحَقِّ مِنَ الَّذِينَ أُوتُوا الْكِتَابَ حَتَّىٰ يُعْطُوا الْجِزْيَةَ عَن يَدٍ وَهُمْ صَاغِرُونَ" **9:29**, the Messenger called Medina people and the surrounding Arabs to Jihad (seeking the path to God), informing them that they would attack the Romans. This was in Rajab, 9 AH. Every battle or expedition the Messenger was intending, he was keeping it secret. Yet this was not the case with Tabouk, as he announced it, so that the Muslims could be prepared for the fierce and great army of their enemy. He did so, after harvest in a barren year. Thereafter the Muslims get prepared for the battle.

Othman ibn Afan spent a lot of money over this army, that was named (Alusra). He spent about a thousand dinars. Some said: he brought a thousand horses and a thousand steeds. He well-prepared the army.

The army moved in about thirty-thousand fighters, Medina was left under the guardianship of Mohamed ibn Maslama, some said: it was Sibaa ibn Orfuta. Others said: but Ali ibn Abu Talib. The fact is that Ali was responsible to guard the women and children, but Ali got surprised: saying "Do you want to leave me with the children and women?" The Messenger said, "Will you not be pleased that you will be to me like Aaron to Moses? But there will be no prophet after me."

Abdullah ibn Abu ibn Saloul moved with him, but he did not complete and returned.

Women and children did not join the Messenger, peace be upon him, and so did men who had not a horses or enough money, they were: Salim ibn Omair, Oulba ibn Zaid, Abu Laila Abdulrahman ibn Kaab, Amr ibn Alhumam, Abdullah ibn Almughfal Almuzny, Harmy ibn Abdullah and Irbad ibn Sarya Alfazary. Besides, about eighty hypocrites did not join the Messenger.

Some disobeyers did not join the Messenger, peace be upon him, such as: Murara ibn Alrabie, Kaab ibn Malik and Hilal ibn Omaya. Yet, they were forgiven fifty days after the Messenger's return.

On his way, the Messenger passed by Alhigr (Thamud's Land)[4], he ordered them not to enter their houses, to drink only from the camel's will, and to get rid of the flour they made by feeding it to the camels. He was masked at that time.

He reached Tabouk, that had a spring with a little water, then increased upon his honorable arrival. He was praying God at that time to grant his army enough water and food. For water, a cloud passed so it rained, so they drank till saturation, this cloud covered the army only.

When he reached there, no war broke out, he considered entry to the Levant in this year is difficult, so he intended return. He made peace with Johnah ibn Roaba, ruler of Ayla (currently Jordanian Aqaba) and sent Khalid ibn Alwalid to Ukidr, king of Dumat Aljandal, so he visited the Messenger and they made peace with each other.

After his return, the Messenger ordered Muslims to demolish Aldirar mosque (Medinan mosque that was erected close to the Quba' Mosque), that was founded from Khizam ibn Khalid's house. Upon the Messenger's order, Malik ibn Aldukhshum, brother of Banu Salim, one of Badr fighters, demolished it. God forbade the Messenger to enter this mosque.

---

[4] is the name of an ancient civilization in the Hejaz known from the 8th century BCE

He returned form such expedition in Ramadan, 9 AH, when Surah of Al-Tawbah was revealed, as God blamed those who absented themselves in the expedition. He said: "It was not [proper] for the people of Madinah and those surrounding them of the bedouins that they remain behind after [the departure of] the Messenger or that they prefer themselves over his self ". " مَا كَانَ لِأَهْلِ الْمَدِينَةِ وَمَنْ حَوْلَهُم مِّنَ الْأَعْرَابِ أَن يَتَخَلَّفُوا عَن رَّسُولِ اللَّهِ وَلَا يَرْغَبُوا بِأَنفُسِهِمْ عَن نَّفْسِهِ".9:120 God also said: "And it is not for the believers to go forth [to battle] all at once. For there should separate from every division of them a group [remaining] to obtain understanding in the religion and warn their people when they return to them that they might be cautious." " وَمَا كَانَ الْمُؤْمِنُونَ لِيَنفِرُوا كَافَّةً ۚ فَلَوْلَا نَفَرَ مِن كُلِّ فِرْقَةٍ مِّنْهُمْ طَائِفَةٌ لِّيَتَفَقَّهُوا فِي الدِّينِ وَلِيُنذِرُوا قَوْمَهُمْ إِذَا رَجَعُوا إِلَيْهِمْ لَعَلَّهُمْ يَحْذَرُونَ" 9:122

Thaqif Delegation

Thaqif sent a delegation to the Messenger, peace be upon him, in Ramadan, in the same year they converted to Islam. The main ground was that their leader Urwa ibn Masoud, came to the Messenger on his departure from Hunayn and Taif, before arrival to Medina, as he converted to Islam. He then asked the Messenger to return to his nation, calling them to worship God, he accepted but he was worried about Urwa. When he returned to his nation, calling them to convert to Islam, he was killed.

However, they so regretted, believing that they cannot bear a war against the Messenger. So, they sent a delegation of six, in

Ramadan. Almughayra ibn Shaaba Althaqfy was the first who saw them, while he was fostering the Messenger's camel. He took them to the Messenger, teaching them how to salute the Messenger. Abu Bakr, may God be pleased with him, came before Almughayra and cheerfully reported their arrival to the Messenger.

They stayed in the mosque, for which a doom was built. The mediator was Khalid ibn Said ibn Alaas. Food was brought to them from the Messenger, but they would not eat till Khalid ate. They converted to Islam, but they declared a condition which was Alat (an idol referred to a goddess they worshipped) will be kept and not demolished. But the Messenger refused. They asked him to have less prayers, but he again refused. They also asked him not to demolish Alat themselves, he accepted. He sent Abu Sufian Sakhr ibn Harab and Almughayra ibn Shaaba to demolish Alat. Women of Thaqif feared this, thinking they would be harmed upon this demolishment. Almughayra mocked of them, pretending that he was harmed by Alat, then he laughs at them. Thus, they later converted to Islam.

The Messenger assigned Othman ibn Abu Alaas upon them who was one of the delegation, he was the youngest, but the Messenger noticed that he was keen on reciting Qur'an and learning the Islamic duties. He ordered Othman to appoint a call prayer, who would manage the prayer according to the weakest prayer's power.

Pilgrimage of Abu Bakr Alsediq, recurrence of delegations and dispatching of messengers

Abu Bakr Alsedik was sent by the Messenger, peace be upon him, as a leader for the pilgrimage company for that year, and he caused Ali to succeed Abu Bakr. He instructed that there is no disbeliever would enter the Kaaba or a naked would circumambulate it. All pacts, but the respected time-framed ones would be rebuffed.

Delegations recurrently came to the Messenger in that year and the following one, converting to Islam, embracing it in masses, as God said: "When the victory of God has come and the conquest, And you see the people entering into the religion of God in multitudes, Then exalt [Him] with praise of your Lord and ask forgiveness of Him. Indeed, He is ever Accepting of repentance". " ذَا جَاءَ نَصْرُ اللَّهِ وَالْفَتْحُ، وَرَأَيْتَ النَّاسَ يَدْخُلُونَ فِي دِينِ اللَّهِ أَفْوَاجًا، "فَسَبِّحْ بِحَمْدِ رَبِّكَ وَاسْتَغْفِرْهُ إِنَّهُ كَانَ تَوَّابًا"110:2

The Messenger sent both Moaz ibn Jabal and Abu Mousa Alashaary to Yemen. He dispatched the messengers to kings of the countries, calling them for worshipping God and converting   to   Islam.

Farewell Sermon

On that Thursday, 6th Zulhija 10 AH Messenger, peace be upon him, performed the Noon Prayer in medina, then moved with his accompanying Medinan and Bedouin Muslims and performed the Afternoon Prayer in Zulhulaifa and stayed there.

While he was in valley of Aqiq, the Messenger was inspired by God, to say in his Sermon that the Umrah could be coupled with the pilgrimage. Then he actually informed the people of that. He then performed two prostrations and performed both pilgrimage and Umrah. So many people moved with him to do the same.

When he reached Mecca, he ritually walked between Mounts Safa and Marwa. He said: "If I had formerly known what I came to know recently, I would not have driven the Hadi (sacrifice) with me and would have finished the state of Ihram along with the people when they finished it."

When Ali returned from Yemen, the Messenger said with (what intention) have you put on Ihram? He said: I have put on Ihram in accordance with the intention with which the Messenger has put on Ihram, whereupon the Messenger said: I brought the sacrifice and performed both pilgrimage and Umrah. This is narrated by Abu Dawood and other Imams.

Then the Messenger went to Mina and stayed there. It was on that Friday, 9th Zulhija. Then, in the morning he directed to Mount Arafat and delivered his Sermon, attended by about forty-thousands of his companions. He combined both Noon and Afternoon Prayers together and waited at Arafat. Thereafter, he directed to Muzdalifah and combined both Sunset and Evening Prayers. At the daybreak, he performed the Dawn Prayer at time.

Before sunrise, he directed to Mina, to perform "stoning of the devil" ritual and slaughtered the sacrifice and got shaved.

Then, he circumambulated performing what is called "Tawaf Alfard". It is not clear where he performed the Noon Prayer on that day. Two days after sacrificing, he delivered a sermon, he warned, recommended and alerted the Muslims, informing them that he delivered the Islam message. He actually delivered the Islam message, and advised his nation. He then directed to Medina.

His death

He stayed there till the end of Zulhija, Almuhram and Safar. Then he started to feel pain in his head when he was at Maymouna's on Thursday, he felt a severe headache. However, he was visiting his wives, but it became uphill. Thus, he asked them to stay at Aisha's to be nursed, they accepted. He stayed there for twelve days, some said but fourteen. He ordered Abu Bakr to lead the Muslims in prayer, as he excluded Abu Bakr from Osama's army prepared to expediate to the Levant, attacking the Romans.

When he felt pain, the army waited, and he, peace be upon him, prayed behind Abu Bakr, sitting.

He passed away at the forenoon of that Monday, 12th Rabi al-awal. He was sixty-three when he died. Abu Bakr, Omar ibn Alkhatab, Ali ibn Abu Talib and Aisha also died when they were sixty-three. Some opinions referred that the Messenger died when he was sixty, others referred to sixty-five. These three opinions are mentioned in Albukhary's Sahih, according to ibn Abbas.

Calamity fell over the Muslims, upon their Prophet's death. For Omar ibn Alkhatab, he denied that saying: The Messenger did not die, but he will return to his people as Moses did. People were excited. His close honest friend whose support to him was unprecedented, Abu Bakr recited: "Muhammad is not but a messenger. [Other] messengers have passed on before him. So, if he was to die or be killed, would you turn back on your heels [to unbelief]? And he who turns back on his heels will never harm God at all; but God will reward the grateful." " وَمَا مُحَمَّدٌ إِلَّا رَسُولٌ قَدْ خَلَتْ مِن قَبْلِهِ الرُّسُلُ ۚ أَفَإِن مَّاتَ أَوْ قُتِلَ انقَلَبْتُمْ عَلَىٰ أَعْقَابِكُمْ ۚ وَمَن يَنقَلِبْ عَلَىٰ عَقِبَيْهِ فَلَن يَضُرَّ اللَّهَ شَيْئًا ۗ وَسَيَجْزِي اللَّهُ الشَّاكِرِينَ"3:144

People did not hear such verse before, so all of them began to recite it. Muslims then directed with Abu Bakr to Saqifa (roofed building) of Banu Saada and agreed to assign Saad ibn Obada as a successor to rule the Muslims, but he so refused, suggesting Omar ibn Alkhatab or Abu Obaida ibn Algarah, then, Muslims and God so refused. Muslims pledged obedience to him on the pulpit.

Some started to wash his clothed body. His uncle Alabbas, his son Qutham, Ali ibn Abu Talib, Osama ibn Zaid and Shuqran. Aws ibn Khouly Alansary Albadry was there also assisting.

They shrouded the Messenger's body with three white unsewn cotton garments.

Many performed the Funeral Prayer (a prayer performed in congregation to seek pardon for the dead Muslim), one by one. According to a narration by the Messenger mentioned by Albazar, the Messenger himself ordered so. Nonpareils performed the Funeral Prayer, more than once, for his mightiness, they were competing over leading such prayer. Alhakim Abu Ahmed said: first of them was his uncle Alabbas, then Banu Hashim, immigrants, Ansar and the rest of people. When men finished performing the prayers, they were followed by children and women.

He was buried on Tuesday, some opinions referred to Wednesday, in the same place where he died at Aisha's, which is now inside Alnabawi mosque.

The Messenger's pilgrimage and Umrah

The Messenger performed only one pilgrimage, it is called the Islam pilgrimage and the farewell pilgrimage. The pilgrimage was imposed as a religious duty in 6 AH, according to some scholars and in 9 AH according to others. A bizarre opinion referred that it was imposed in 10 AH. A more bizarre opinion referred that the pilgrimage was imposed before immigration.

For his Umrahs, they were four: that of Hudaybiyya, which he is driven away from, Umrah of Alqadaa, Umrah of Aljurana and that last one, which was coupled with his pilgrimage.

The Messenger performed a pilgrimage before immigration. It was said but more than one pilgrimage, this is the common opinion, as he was going there in the pilgrimage occasion, calling people to worship God

CHAPTER 25

Number of his battles and expeditions

For his battles and expeditions, Imam Muslim said according to Abdullah ibn Burida ibn Alhasib Alaslami: The Messenger's expeditions were eleven and his battles were eight. Yet Zaid ibn Arqam said: his battles and expeditions were nineteen, I joined him in seven. Mohamed ibn Isaac said: battles he initiated himself were twenty-seven, his expeditions were thirty-eight.

His prophecy signs

➤ The most glamorous sign is the honorable Qur'an, which is absolutely true, revealed by God to achieve a miracle in both wording and meaning:

For wording, it reaches the highest eloquence levels. It challenged the most eloquent and articulate people at the time of revelation, as they were severely opposing and accusing it of falsehood. God challenged them to form a similar book or at least a part of it, as they were famous for their eloquent poems, but they could not. God challenged all his creatures from human and Jinn to form a similar book, yet they could not. He said: " Say, "If mankind and the jinn gathered in order to produce the like of this Qur'an, they could not produce the like of it, even if they were to each other assistants." " قُل لَّئِنِ اجْتَمَعَتِ الْإِنسُ

وَالْجِنُّ عَلَىٰ أَن يَأْتُوا بِمِثْلِ هَٰذَا الْقُرْآنِ لَا يَأْتُونَ بِمِثْلِهِ وَلَوْ كَانَ بَعْضُهُمْ لِبَعْضٍ ظَهِيرًا"17:88

For its meanings, Qur'an implies these meanings of collaboration, wisdom, mercy, good and agreement. Only the wise can deduce such meanings.

> He grew in a nation that knew his ancestry, and sensed his credibility and honesty, his benefaction and reason. All of them know that, except the trivial and opponents. He was ignorant, did not how to write. He came to his nation, when he was forty, to call them to God. He was considered of being honest and loyal. He was devoting himself and his time to God, worshipping, praying, humbling and invocating to God. He was featured with his good morals, such as generosity, courage, modesty and benevolence…etc. Thus, it is logical that this man cannot be a liar. Only lies are told by those evil-minded and foxy people.

> He was also featured by knowing the unseen that later corresponded the reality.

> God privileged him with some wonders and miraculous powers. When disbelievers asked him to show them a prodigy, he pointed to the moon, so it split. They asked the surrounding people, lest they should be bewitched, yet they indicated the truth of the moon splitting.

➤ His accepted invocations that brought abundance in too many places. Such cases cannot be listed briefly. However, Alhafiz Abu Bakr Albehqy wrote a book in this regard: He asked God to increase the milk of the lamb of ibn Masoud, so it watered him and Abu Bakr. The same happened with the sheep of Om Maabad. He asked God to grant Altufail ibn Amr Aldawsy light, so a wonderful light emerged in his whip end.

He asked God to take revenge from the seven who mocked of him, while he was praying, so they were killed in the battle of Badr.

He also asked God to take revenge from ibn Abu Lahab, so he was caught by a dog in the Levant, complying with the Messenger's invocation.

For Suraqa, he asked God to avoid him his evil, so limbs of his steed sank in the sands. He threw the disbelievers of Quraish in Badr with a handful of pebbles. All of them were afflicted and defeated. And he did the same in Hunayn.

On the day of battle of Badr, the Messenger gave Ukasha ibn Mihsan a piece of firewood, which turned into a sharp sword.

He also informed his uncle, Alabbas – while he was a captive – of the money he and his wife buried under their house door, he admitted so to the Messenger, peace be upon him.

The Messenger showed Omair ibn Wahb up, telling him that he knew his intention (to kill the Messenger), and that Omair falsely justified his coming as he wanted to check Badr's captives. Omair so admitted and converted to Islam.

On the day of Uhud, he healed eye of Qatada ibn Al-noaman Alzafry, after being injured and oozed. It became identical to the other, as if nothing happened.

On the day of the Trench, he managed to feed the big masses of his army, which was about a thousand fighters, from only one lamb. Daughter of Bashir also brought a handful of dates, yet such inconsiderable handful was a big meal.

He also could feed about eighty men from a food too little to appear in his hand. The same happened when he married Zainab bint Gahsh. On the day of Tabouk, he fed the army and kept too much food, just from small amount of food equals to a goat. These are just a few examples, yet the Messenger's similar incidents are a lot.

➢ He also asked God, on aridity to grant them water. He did not leave the pulpit till water dropped on his beard from the mosque ceiling.

He asked God to take revenge from Quraish, so they received unprecedented storm and winds, till they asked him for mercy, and he released and saved them.

He brought a bowl of water to perform ablution, thus people wanted to perform ablution too. He put his hand in the bowl, and it got wider, then water was running between his fingers.

On the day of Hudaybiyya, he did the same with his thousand-and-four-hundred-fighter army. Jabir said: if we would a hundred thousand, water would be enough.

He did so several times. A man said when the Messenger ordered me to put water in a bowl, it was too little to even appear in it, he put his hand in the bowl, the water run between his fingers, so that they could perform ablution and drink.

Another example for his bless is when the Messenger shot the will of Hudaybiyya, so it exploded flowing water till saturation. The same happened with the woman of the two water sinks, as his companions drank and performed ablution, yet water remained the same. The woman returned to her nation, saying: I saw the world's greatest magicians, he is a prophet. She converted to Islam and so did her nation."

CHAPTER 27

Telling of the Unseen

The Messenger, peace be upon him, was able to tell the unseen events, which was or became later true, as God inspired him of that. He foresaw the Romans victory over the Persians.

He told his people that God was sending white ants to eat the leaf written by the disbelievers, except God's name, this was true.

One day before Badr, he foresaw the murdered, naming them one by one.

He knew and foretold that treasures of Khosrow of Persia and Caesar of Rome will be spent seeking the path to God and for His cause. His words came to reality.

He heralded his nation that their kingdom will stretch across the world. This later became real.

Surprisingly, the Messenger, peace be upon him, foretold that his nation would fight a nation whose people are narrow-eyed and small-nosed. These are the traits of Tatars.

He forecasted the Khawarij fighting and typically described Zalthudia (Hirqous ibn Zuhair al-Bajali).

He managed to foretell that Alhasan ibn Ali would make peace between two Muslim groups (The Levant and Iraq)

He forecasted that Amar ibn Yasser would be killed by his enemy, so he was murdered in the battle of Siffin. (It was a fight between Ali ibn Abu Talib who ruled as the Fourth Caliph and Muawiyah I, on the banks of the Euphrates river, currently Raqqa, Syria.)

He foretold that a fire would come from Saudi Arabia that shed light on the necks of the camels at Busra. This was happened in 654 AH - 1256 BC as the lava flowed from Harrat Rahat in Medina where it erupted for about 3 months.

Earlier Holy Books foresaw the Messenger

God announced in both Torah and Bible that Muhammad would be revealed. God so told his Prophet Jesus as: "bringing good tidings of a messenger to come after me, whose name is Ahmad". **61:6** "وَمُبَشِّرًا بِرَسُولٍ يَأْتِي مِن بَعْدِي اسْمُهُ أَحْمَدُ". Albukhary said, according to Abdullah ibn Amr that Muhammad was described in Torah.

In Torah, the first apocalyptic contains that God inspired Abraham saying what it means: "Be proud of your son". It is known that nobody, but Muhammad's nation was spreading in great spaces across the world. In Sahih of Imam Muslim, the Messenger was quoted saying: "Verily, God drew the ends of the world near me until I saw its east and west, my nation will reach as far as I saw".

In Torah, "And as for Ishmael, I have heard thee: Behold, I have blessed him, and will make him fruitful, and will multiply him exceedingly; twelve princes shall he beget, and I will make him a great nation, which will be honored by the great Muhammad"

God promised Abraham that his son Ishmael will have the upper hand above all nations. Christians and Jews knew that Ishmael did not enter the Levant, but it was Muhammad.

In the Torah Deuteronomy, God said: "A prophet from their relatives, just like you, Moses". They know that God did not reveal a prophet from Ishmael's decedents except Muhammad. For Israeli people, only Jesus was a prophet like Moses, yet they did not acknowledge his prophecy, and he did not belong to their siblings. Jesus, peace be upon him, is related to them only from Mother. What is meant only applies to Muhammad.

At the end of Torah, in Deuteronomy, God said: " The LORD came from Sinai and dawned over them from Seir; He shone forth from Mount Paran". This implies that God's law came from Mount Sinai on which He talked to Moses, emerges from Mount Seir, where Jesus was born and develops form Mount Paran, which is Mecca, as God ordered Abraham to take Ishmael to Mount Paran. Some scholars quoted God's words, to prove the truthfulness of this. God said in Qur'an: "By the fig and the olive, And [by] Mount Sinai, And [by] this secure city [Mecca]". "وَالتِّينِ وَالزَّيْتُونِ وَطُورِ سِينِينَ وَهَذَا الْبَلَدِ الْأَمِينِ" 95:1-3

In Torah, God referred to his prophets, according to their locations. In Qur'an, He swore by these spots as mentioned Jesus home, then Moses's and Muhammad's.

Dawood's scriptures and prophecies existing in the Bible and Torah contained glad tidings about the Messenger, peace be upon him.

In Bible, Paraclete was mentioned, described as holding traits and   features   of   Muhammad.

The Messenger's Children

Previously, we discussed ancestry of uncles and aunts of the Messenger.

For his children, males and females were born by his wife Khadija, only Ibrahim was born by Maria Alqibteya, his children were:

Alqasem, the Messenger was called (Abul Alqasem – father of Alqasem) as he was his oldest children, Zeinab, Roqaia, Om Kalthoum and Fatima.

After revelation and prophecy, he begot Abdulla, who was called Altayb and Altaher (the kind and the virtuous), as he was born after Islam.

Ibrahim, son of Maria, born in Medina in 8 AH and died when he was a year and ten months. Of him, the Messenger said: "There is a wet-nurse for him in Paradise."

All of his children died before him, except Fatima, may God be pleased with her, she died shortly after his father's death. Some said: after six months, this is the common opinion. Others said: eight months. Some opinions referred that they were seventy days or seventy-five days. Other opinions referred to three months, or a hundred days.

Ali ibn Abu Talib performed the Funeral Prayer over her. Some said it was Abu Bakr, but it is a bizarre opinion. In a narration, it was said that she washed shortly before her death and bequeathed that she would not be washed after her death, yet this is odd.

It was said that Ali, Alabbas, Asmaa bint Amis, wife of Abu Bakr and Salma Om Rafi washed her. This opinion is common.

His Wives

His first wife was Khadija bint Khuwaylid. She was a believer in him. In her life, she was his only wife, being his very thing. It was controverted which was closer to the Messenger, peace be upon him, Khadija or Aisha? It was likely Khadija. She died a year and half before Hijrah (immigration to Medina).

He then married to Sawda bint Zamaa Alquraishya Alamerya in Mecca, after Khadija's death.

It was said that he married to Aisha before Sawda, she was the only virgin he married. He loved her the most. She had special traits and features mentioned in Qur'an and narrations. She was the most educated woman about her religion. She died in 57 or 58 AH.

He then married Hafsa, daughter of Omar ibn Alkhatab, in 3 AH, he divorced her but then take her back. In 41 AH, she died. Some said it was in 50 AH and others said but in 45 AH.

Later, the Messenger, peace be upon him, married Om Salma, (Hind bint Huthaifa Abu Omaya), after death of her husband Abu Salma (Abdullah ibn Abd Alasad ibn Hilal ibn Abdullah ibn Makhzoum). He proposed to her after the "waiting period for a widow". This was in the beginning of 3 AH. Her proxy was her son Omar, as narrated by Alnisaey, according to Hamad ibn Salma, on behalf of Thabet Albunany. Alwaqidy said that her proxy was her son Salma. This is the more common opinion. Others said that the Messenger married her with no proxy. Al-waqidy said she died in 59 AH. Others said she died during the ruling of Yazid ibn Moawia in 62 AH.

Consequently, he married to Zainab bint Gahsh in Zulqida 5 AH. Other said the marriage was in 3 AH, but this opinion is not trusted. She married him without proxy. God said: "So when Zayd had no longer any need for her, We married her to you". 33:37"فَلَمَّا قَضَىٰ زَيْدٌ مِنْهَا وَطَرًا زَوَّجْنَاكَهَا"

She was boasting as she got married to the Messenger with no proxy but God, unlike the other wives who got married to him under proxy of their families. She was the first wife to die. Al-waqidy said that she died in 20 AH, as Omar ibn Alkhatab performed the Funeral Prayer for her.

Thereafter he married Juayraia (daughter of Alharith ibn Abu Darar) Almustalqia, as when he attacked her nation at Almuray-sie. She was among the booty share of Thabet ibn Qais ibn Shamas, so she came to the Messenger, peace be upon him, asking for help, he then released her and married her. She died in 50 AH. Alwaqidy said: but in 56 AH.

Among his wives was the Israeli Safeya (daughter of Huyay ibn Akhtab) Alharouneya from Nadir. In the battle of Khaybar, she was picked by him from the booty, in the beginning of 7 AH. He released her and this was her dowry. She later wore the Hijab and was called one of the Mothers of believers. Alwaqidy said that she died in 50 AH, other said: but in 36 AH.

In 7 or may be 6 AH, he married to Ramla Om Habiba (daughter of Abu Sufian Sakhr ibn Harb ibn Omaya ibn Abd Shams. Amr ibn Omaya Aldamary interceded this proposal, while she was in Ethiopia, when his husband Obaidullah ibn Gahsh. Alnajashi paid her dowry, instead of the Messenger, which was four hundred Dinars.

Imam Muslim said in his Sahih, according to Akrama ibn Amar Alyamany, on behalf of Abu Zumail Simak ibn Alwalid ibn Abbas; that when Abu Sufian converted to Islam, he said that he had the best and most beautiful Arab woman, Om Habiba, his daughter. He offered the Messenger her marriage. Yet how Muslim did not notice that Abu Sufian just converted to Islam on the conquest of Mecca, as a year or more after the conquest, the Messenger married Om Habiba.

In Zulqida of the same year, he married Maymouna (daughter of Alharith) Alhilalya. It was controverted if he was on pilgrimage or not. Both Sahihs referred according to ibn Abbas that the

Messenger was on pilgrimage. Yet, the Messenger said: "A Muhrim (one in the state of Ihram) must neither marry himself, nor arrange the marriage of another one, nor should he make the proposal of marriage." He did not marry her till he finished his pilgrimage and left Mecca, as he married her in Sarif (currently Nawariyyah). She also died in Sarif in 51 AH. Others said in 53 or 56 AH. Her nephew Abdullah ibn Abbas performed the Funeral Prayer for her.

He had two concubines:

Maria Alqibteya, mother of Ibrahim, son of the Messenger. She was granted to him by Muqawqis, king of Egypt and Alexandra at that time, along with her sister Shereen, a eunuch, called Mabour and a mule called Doldol. The Messenger granted Shereen to Hassan ibn Thabet, begetting Abdulrahman. Maria died in Almuhram 16 AH. Omar ibn Alkhatab was gathering people to perform the Funeral Prayer for her, then he buried her in Albaqi.

The second was Rihanna (his father was called Amr or Zayd), she was selected by the Messenger from Banu Qurayza. Some said that he married her, but she was only her bondmaid. Later he released her and returned to her nation.[5]

His Valets

Here is an enumeration of the Messenger's valets. They were Ahmar (called Abu Asib), Aswad, Aflah, Anas, Ayman, Bazam, Thawban ibn Bogdud, Zakwan (some called him Tahman), Kisan (some called him Marawan, and Mahran), Rafie, Rabah, Rofai, Zaid ibn Haritha, Zaid, grandfather of Hilal ibn Yasar, Sabiq, Salim, Said, Safina, Salman Alfarsi, Salim (called Abu Kabsha, he attended Badr), Saleh (Shuqran), Dumaira, Fadala Alyamany, Qusair, Kirkira, Mabour, Midaam, Maymoun, Nafie, Nabil, Harmaz, Hisham, Waqid, Werdan, Yasar, Abu Athila, Abu Bakra, Abu Ahamraa, Abu Rafie (some called him Aslam and Abu Obaid).

These valets were mentioned by Abu Zakaria Alnawawy, in the beginning of his book (Tahzib Alasmaa wal Loghat "Refinement of Names and Languages).

His bondmaids were: Omaya, Baraka (mother of Ayman and Osama ibn Zayd), Khedra, Radwa, Rihanna, Salma (mother of

Rafie), Shereen, Maria Alqibteya, Maymouna bint Saad, Om Damira (Mother of Damira) and Om Ayash (Mother of Ayash).

Abu Zakaria said: he did not possess them all at one time but over time.

His Attendants

Some of the companions wanted to be at his service. Abdullah ibn Masoud was keen on his shoes. If the Messenger stood up, Abdullah attired him his shoes, if he sat down, Abdullah was carrying them. Almughayra ibn Shaaba was his guard. Oqba ibn Amer was bridling his mule in his travels. His attendants included also Anas ibn Malik, Rabiaa ibn Kaab, Bilal and Zu Makhbar (also called Zu Makhmar, nephew of Alnajashi, king of Ethiopia.

CHAPTER 32

Scribes of the Revelation

For the scribes of the revelation, they were Abu Bakr, Omar ibn Alkhatab, Othman ibn Afan, Ali ibn Abu Talib, Alzubair, Abu ibn Kaab, Zayd ibn Thabet, Moawia ibn Abu Sufian, Mohammed ibn Muslima, Alarqam ibn Abu Alarqam, Aban ibn Said ibn Alaas, his brother Khalid, Thabet ibn Qais, Hanzala ibn Alrabie Alasidy, Khalid ibn Alwalid, Abdullah ibn Alarqam, Abdullah ibn Zayd ibn Abdrabu, Alalaa ibn Otba, Almughayra ibn Shaaba, Sharhabel ibn Hasna. Alhafiz Abu Alqasem mentioned this in his book and gathered proofs for all of them, except Sharhabel.

Prayer callers

He had four prayer callers: Bilal ibn Rabah, Omar ibn Om Maktoum (also called Abdullah), they were shifting calling for prayers in Medina, Saad Alqaraz in Qibaa and Abu Mahzoura in Mecca.

His camels and horses

His camels called Aladbaa, Algadaa and Alqaswaa. Mohamed ibn Ibrahim Altamimy said: The Messenger had only one camel with these three names.

His horses called Alsakb, he was beautifully white-footed. It was the first horse he battled on. Another horse was called Sabha, which he used in race. Almurtgez was that sold to him by a Bedouin and Khazima ibn Thabet witnessed such sale. Sahl ibn Saad said: he had three steeds: Lizaz, Alzarb and Allakhif. Another one was called Alward, which he was granted by Tamim Aldary.

He had a mule called Doldol, granted by Muqawqis, used by him in Hunayn. It long lasted after him, till it was fed the barley as liquid, out of losing its teeth. It was adopted by Ali ibn Abu Talib and then by Abdullah ibn Gaefer. Moreover, he had a donkey called Oufair.

A strange tale was narrated in this regard by Abu Qasim Alsahily, that the donkey talked to the Messenger informing him that it was descended from seventy donkeys, each was ridden by a prophet, and that its name was Yazid ibn Shihab. The Messenger used to send Oufair to his companions, when needed. Yet it was not true, but only according to Mohamed ibn Abu Hatem who relied on untrusted sources. The Messenger at some time owned twenty camels that produce much milk and a hundred sheep.

His weapons

From the war weapons, he had three lances, three bows and six swords, of them is Zulfuqar, which he used in Badr, an armor, a shield, a ring, a goblet, a squared black flag and white banner.

Sending delegates to kings

He sent Amr ibn Omaya Aldamry to Alnajashi, holding a message calling for Islam. So, he converted to Islam.

He sent Deheya ibn Khalifa Alkalby to Hercules of Rome. He was about to convert to Islam, but he did not. Some said he did. Sunaid ibn Dawood brought an incompletely transmitted narration, supporting that he converted to Islam. Abu Obaid narrated in his book (Alamwal) an incompletely transmitted narration, supporting that he did not.

He sent Abdullah ibn Huthafa Alsahmy to Khosrow of Persia, yet he behaved arrogantly and tore the message.

Furthermore, Hateb ibn Abu Baltaa was sent by the Messenger to Muqawqis of Alexandria and Egypt. He welcomed but did not convert to Islam but sent gifts to the Messenger.

Amr ibn Alaas was sent to kings of Oman, who both converted to Islam.

Sulait ibn Amr Alamry was sent to Hawza ibn Ali Alhanafy at Alyamama (at the east of the plateau of Najd in modern-day Saudi Arabia)

He sent Shogaa ibn Wahb Alasady to Alharith ibn Abu Shamr Alghasany of Balqa in the Levant.

Almuhajir ibn Abu Omaya Almakhzoumy was sent to Alharith Alhemery.

Alalaa ibn Alhadremy was sent to Almounzir ibn Sawa Alabdi of Bahrain, and he converted to Islam.

Abu Mousa Alashaary and Moaz ibn Jabal were sent to Yemen, as its rulers and people converted to Islam.

His appearance

For his appearance, Imam Abu Eisa Mohamed ibn Eisa ibn Sura Alturmuzy was the best who talked about this in his book (Kitab Alshamael "Book of Merits"), followed by the Scholars and Imams, he supported his writings with evidence. Such was explained in detail by Alhafiz Abu Alqasim ibn Asaker and Alhafiz Abu Alhajaj Almizay in (Tahzib Alkamal). Abu Zakaria Alnawawy briefly talked about the Messenger's appearance. He cleared that:

The Messenger, peace be upon him, was medium-heighted, with medium-tanned skin and slightly curled hair.

Until his death, hoariness did not gig his head. The Messenger was fit and Broad-shouldered. His hair was of shoulder length. In another time, it was ear length. His face was prinked by a bushy beard. His hands were coarse. His metaphyses were big. His rounded-head was sizable, with black, long-lashed red-tear-ducted eyes. His steps were stable and strong. His voice was kind. He had smooth checks and wide, neat-teethed mouth. His chest and stomach were flat. Hair covered his shoulders, arms and upper chest. His forearms were long with ample palms. He was skinny-ankled.

He was unloosing his hair, combing his beard, darkening his eyelids with kohl every night before sleep.

For clothes, he was preferring the shirt, white clothes and wraps. His shirt sleeve was reaching his wrist. At some time, he was wearing a red costume, a below-waist loin cloth and a garment. At other time, he was wearing two green garments. He was also seen wearing an overcoat with tight sleeves and a wrap. Sometimes he was wearing a black turban, unloosing its ends on shoulders. Some saw him wearing a black robe, a ring, sandals or shoes.

Anas ibn Malik said: I have never touched a silk softer than the Messenger's hands or smelled a perfume more pleasant than the Messenger's. I was assisting the Messenger, peace be upon him, for ten years, and he never rebuked or blamed me.

Abdullah ibn Salam said: when the Messenger, peace be upon him, came to Medina, people hurtled to him, when I look at him, I recognized that he was not a liar.

His good morals

Concerning his good morals, God said: "Nun. By the pen and what they inscribe, You are not, [O Muhammad], by the favor of your Lord, a madman. And indeed, for you is a reward uninterrupted. And indeed, you are of a great moral character." " ن وَالْقَلَمِ وَمَا يَسْطُرُونَ. مَا أَنتَ بِنِعْمَةِ رَبِّكَ بِمَجْنُونٍ. وَإِنَّ لَكَ لَأَجْرًا غَيْرَ مَمْنُونٍ. وَإِنَّكَ لَعَلَى خُلُقٍ عَظِيمٍ" 68:1-4

Aisha said that the Messenger's morals were complying with Qur'an. This means that he committed himself to obey God. In Qur'an, he said: " Indeed, this Qur'an guides to that which is most suitable" " إِنَّ هَٰذَا الْقُرْآنَ يَهْدِي لِلَّتِي هِيَ أَقْوَمُ" 17:9

He was the bravest at the war perils.

He was the most generous, specially in Ramadan (the month of fasting)

He was the most obeying, the most eloquent, the best consultant and the most patient.

He was the most honorable. When he entered Mecca on the day of conquest, he bowed his head out of humbleness.

He was so shy, but he was the strongest, concerning the religion. He was quoted saying: "I am the mortal bright-faced".

God praised him and his companions, saying: "Muhammad is the Messenger of God; and those with him are forceful against the disbelievers, merciful among themselves." " مُحَمَّدٌ رَّسُولُ اللَّهِ ۚ 48:29"وَالَّذِينَ مَعَهُ أَشِدَّاءُ عَلَى الْكُفَّارِ رُحَمَاءُ بَيْنَهُمْ

His journeys

• He visited the Levant twice:

The first was with his uncle, Abu Talib, for the purpose of trade, he was only twelve at that time, when Behira the monk brought good tidings about his great rank, based on the miraculous signs he noticed in him. This is mentioned in detail in a narration by Alturmuzy, which also mentioned the shadowing cloud tale, but it was not mentioned in any other narration.

The second journey was for the purpose of trade to Khadija. He reached Busra, for selling and trade. There, her valet Maisra noticed him and his prophecy signs, so he informed his mistress of him. She was willing to marry him, and she really did, when he was only twenty-five.

• We previously talked about his night journey from Alharam mosque to Alaqsa mosque where he led the prophets in prayers. He mounted to the heaven, till the seventh, as he saw the ranks of all prophets there. Then, the Buraq took him to Sidrat Almuntaha, a Lote tree that marks the end of the seventh heaven, where he saw Jibril as God created him, he had six-hundred wings. He came too close from God, seeing his divinity signs, "He certainly saw of the greatest signs of his Lord." " لَقَدْ رَأَىٰ مِنْ آيَاتِ رَبِّهِ الْكُبْرَىٰ" 53:18

Imam Muslim said that he did not see him but only felt Him (His existence). Aisha bint Abu Bakr, may God be pleased with hey, denied that the Messenger saw God. Imam Muslim in his Sahih, according to Qatada, on behalf of Abdullah ibn Shaqiq, and Abu Zar, narrated: " I asked the Messenger of God: Did you see thy Lord? He said: (He is) Light; how could I see Him?".

He saw the Heaven and Hell. God instructed him about the fifty prayers, but the Messenger interceded, so they became the daily five prayers. He also visited Moses, and descended to the Earth, at Alharam mosque in Mecca, telling people what he saw.

Anas ibn Malik quoted the Messenger saying: "I was then brought a white beast which is called Al-Buraq, bigger than a donkey and smaller than a mule. Its stride was as long as the eye could reach. I and Jibril mounted on it, and then we went forth till we reached the lowest heaven, then I was ordered to pray, I obeyed, Jibril said: do you know where you prayed? I said: No, but God knows. Jibril said: In Yathrib, in Tiba. Then, I was ordered to pray, I obeyed, Jibril said: do you know where you prayed? I said: No, but God knows. Jibril said: on Sinai Mount, where God talked to Moses. Then I was ordered to pray, I obeyed, Jibril said: do you know where you prayed? I said: No, but God knows. Jibril said: In Bethlehem where Jesus was born and then entered Jerusalem, where all prophets were gathered and led by me in prayer.

Another narration by ibn Jarir, on behalf of Abu Nuaim, Moqatel ibn Hayan, Aakrama and ibn Abbas, pointed that he was taken at the night to Gog and Magog calling them to worship God, but they refused. Then he was taken to Jablak in the east, whose people were attributed to Aad and the believers thereof and then to Jabers in the west, whose people were attributed to Thamud and the believers thereof. He called peoples of both cities to worship God and they responded. The narration referred that each city had ten-thousand gates, every two are three-mile distant. On every gate ten-thousand guards are located till the doomsday.

His revelations

We previously talked about that the Messenger, peace be upon him, had listened to his God and his speech at the night he was sent to the Heaven, he explained that God said: " O' Muhammad, I have decreed My Obligation and have reduced the burden on My slaves, My orders cannot be cancelled. They are five and they are fifty". These words said only by God, as in Qur'an: "Indeed, I am God. There is no deity except Me, so worship Me and establish prayer for My remembrance.". " إِنَّنِي أَنَا اللَّهُ لَا إِلَٰهَ إِلَّا أَنَا فَاعْبُدْنِي وَأَقِمِ الصَّلَاةَ لِذِكْرِي"20:14

So, scholars agreed that these words cannot be said by anyone but God. It cannot be said by a human to call another for worshipping.

The Messenger, peace be upon him, quoted God saying: "My servants, all of you are hungry, except whom I feed…" This narration was mentioned by Muslim, and the significance is contained in other narrations.

Some Hadith scholars adopted that all ordinances (Hadith) are of revelations and inspirations, as God said in Qur'an: "Nor does he speak from [his own] inclination, It is not but a revelation revealed" "وَمَا يَنطِقُ عَنِ الْهَوَىٰ، إِنْ هُوَ إِلَّا وَحْيٌ يُوحَىٰ"53 : 2-3

He saw Jibril in the form God created him, and he previously saw him descending from the Heaven in the same form, at the beginning of the revelation. In this regard, God said: "Taught to him by one intense in strength, One of soundness. And he rose to [his] true form, While he was in the higher [part of the] horizon, Then he approached and descended, And was at a distance of two bow lengths or nearer." " عَلَّمَهُ شَدِيدُ الْقُوَىٰ، ذُو مِرَّةٍ فَاسْتَوَىٰ " "وَهُوَ بِالْأُفُقِ الْأَعْلَىٰ، ثُمَّ دَنَا فَتَدَلَّىٰ، فَكَانَ قَابَ قَوْسَيْنِ أَوْ أَدْنَى 53:4 - 9

The descender referred to therein is Jibril, according to the Qur'an interpreters. Aisha also so supported as when she asked the Messenger about who was the descender, he said: He is Jibril.

We said above that he met the prophets and recognized their ranks and saw Malik (the angel of Hell) and Ridwan (the angel of Heaven "the Paradise"). Angels of each heaven were welcoming him, sending him to the next one.

In a narration, he said: "On the night when I was taken to the Heaven, I passed by any angels who said to me: "O Muhammad, tell your nation to use cupping.""

Jibril was sent to the Messenger holding Qur'an. In Muslim's Sahih, it is said that an angel was sent holding the last two verses of Surah of Al-Baqrah.

Quotations

His companions quoted him when he was in Mecca, Medina, Arafat, Mina and other places he went to.

Jinn heard him reciting Qur'an in Okaz (an open-air market, near Ta'if, in Saudi Arabia at the epoch of Pre-Islam). So, a fraction of the Jinn embraced Islam.

Jibril appeared to the Messenger, in a form of a Bedouin Man, talking to him about Islam, faith, charity and portents of the doomsday.

Number of Muslims till his death and his narrating companions

On the Messenger's death, Muslims were sixty thousand, thirty thousand were in Medina and the rest were spreading in other places.

Alhafiz Abu Zaraa Obaidallah ibn Abdulkarim Alrazy said: Over a thousand were seeing the Messenger and hearing his recitation till his death.

Alhafiz Abu Abdullah Mohamed ibn Abd Alhakam Alnisaboury said: About four-thousand companions were quoting the Messenger's narrations.

Imams managed to list names of the Companions, such as Albukhary, ibn Abu Khithma, Alhafiz ibn Abu Abdullah ibn Manda, Alhafiz ibn Abu Naim Alasbahany and Imam Abu Amr ibn Abdulbir.

Characteristics of the Messenger

Characteristics are subdivided into two categories:

The first category: He was marked by some characteristics, not found in other prophets, peace be upon them.

The second category: What is peculiar to him and not his nation

First Category

Characteristics not found in other prophets but only him

In both Sahihs, according to Jabir ibn Abdullah ibn Amr ibn Haram Alansary, the Messenger said: "I have been given five things which were not given to anyone else before me. -1. God made me victorious by awe, (frightening my enemies) for a distance of one-month journey. -2. The earth has been made for me (and for my followers) a place for praying therefore anyone of my followers can pray wherever the time of a prayer is due. -3. The booty has been made Halal (lawful) for me yet it was not lawful for anyone else before me. -4. I have been given the right of intercession. -5. Every Prophet used to be sent to his nation only but I have been sent to all mankind"

• In "God made me victorious by awe, (frightening my enemies) for a distance of one-month journey", the Messenger means that if he planned to take an expedition to a nation, they would be frightened of him, a month before his arrival. This was his distinctive feature.

• "The earth has been made for me (and for my followers) a place for praying therefore anyone of my followers can pray wherever the time of a prayer is due" refers to the narration mentioned by Imam Ahmed: "Who were before us did not pray in their houses but in churches". The Messenger also refers that the "Tayamum – ablution with sand or dust" was not allowed to any nation before but was only allowed to the Messenger, peace be upon him, and his nation, out of God's mercy.

• Concerning "The booty has been made Halal (lawful) for me", it was before the Messenger that when booties were distributed, a fire was sent from the sky to burn the shares.

• For "I have been given the right of intercession", the Messenger referred to the special rank God gave him. It was the role of intercession, as on the doomsday, the Messenger will intercede for the people, so God will forgive them. He will enter the Heaven before anyone, so he will intercede for all people to enter the Heaven with him. This is the primary intercession, peculiar only to him, thereafter come other intercessions, as he will save the great sinners of his nations from the Hell. This intercession is shared with other prophets who will intercede for their sinners. In a narration mentioned by Abu Hurayrah, quoting the Messenger saying: "God said: "The angels have interceded, the prophets have interceded, and the believers have interceded, and no one remains (to grant pardon) but the Most Merciful.""

Albukhary in his Sahih, in the Book of Zakat said, on behalf of Yehia ibn Bakir, Allayth, Obaidullah ibn Abu Gaefer, Hamza ibn Abdullah ibn Omar, quoting the Messenger: "A man who persists in begging people to give him charity, will come on the doomsday and there will not be a piece of flesh on his face." He also said: "On the doomsday, the sun will come near (to, the people) to such an extent that the sweat will reach up to the middle of the ears, so, when all the people are in that state, they will ask Adam for help, and then Moses, and then Muhammad".

The sub-narrator added: "Muhammad will intercede to judge amongst the people. He will proceed on till he will hold the ring of the door (of Heaven) and then God will exalt him to "Maqam Mahmud" (the privilege of intercession, etc.). And all the people will send their praises to God". Hence, this is the great intercession, as people will move from a prophet to another till end with Muhammad to judge them.

There are other four intercessions. One is to get back those who entered the Hell. Another is that he will be intercessor in the Heaven, as Anas ibn Malik said, quoting the Messenger: "I am the first intercessor in the Heaven", he will intercede to uplift ranks of some Heaven people. This intercession is supported by both Sunnis and Mutazila (a rationalist school of Islamic theology, that flourished in the cities of Basra and Baghdad, both now in Iraq). Such was supported in Albukhary's Sahih, as when Abu Amer, uncle of Abu Mousa was killed in Autas, the Messenger said: "O' God, forgive Obaid Abu Amer and upgrade him over many of Your human creatures on the doomsday. He also said when Abu Salma ibn Abd Alasad died: "O' God upgrade him".

• Relating "Every Prophet used to be sent to his nation only but I have been sent to all mankind", it is supported and explained in Qur'an, "And We did not send any messenger except [speaking] in the language of his people to state clearly for them", " وَمَا أَرْسَلْنَا مِن رَّسُولٍ إِلَّا بِلِسَانِ قَوْمِهِ لِيُبَيِّنَ لَهُمْ ۖ فَيُضِلُّ اللَّهُ مَن يَشَاءُ وَيَهْدِي مَن يَشَاءُ ۚ وَهُوَ الْعَزِيزُ الْحَكِيمُ"14:4

"And there was no nation but that there had passed within it a warner.","وَإِن مِّنْ أُمَّةٍ إِلَّا خَلَا فِيهَا نَذِيرٌ"35:24

The prophets preceding Muhammad had a mission which is calling only their nations to worship God. Yet, for Muhmmed, peace be upon him; God said:

"Say, [O Muhammad], "O mankind, indeed I am the Messenger of God to you all, [from Him]", " قُلْ يَا أَيُّهَا النَّاسُ إِنِّي رَسُولُ اللَّهِ إِلَيْكُمْ جَمِيعًا"7:158

"And this Qur'an was revealed to me that I may warn you thereby and whomever it reaches.", " وَأُوحِيَ إِلَيَّ هَٰذَا الْقُرْآنُ لِأُنذِرَكُم بِهِ وَمَن بَلَغَ"6:19

"But whoever disbelieves in it from the [various] factions - the Fire is his promised destination", " وَمَن يَكْفُرْ بِهِ مِنَ الْأَحْزَابِ فَالنَّارُ مَوْعِدُهَ" 11:17

"And say to those who were given the Scripture and [to] the unlearned, "Have you embraced Islam? And if they embraced Islam, they are rightly guided; but if they turn away - then upon you is only the [duty of] notification. And God is Seeing of [His] servants. ", " فَإِنْ حَاجُّوكَ فَقُلْ أَسْلَمْتُ وَجْهِيَ لِلَّهِ وَمَنِ اتَّبَعَنِ وَقُل لِّلَّذِينَ أُوتُوا الْكِتَابَ وَالْأُمِّيِّينَ أَأَسْلَمْتُمْ فَإِنْ أَسْلَمُوا فَقَدِ اهْتَدَوا وَّإِن تَوَلَّوْا فَإِنَّمَا عَلَيْكَ الْبَلَاغُ وَاللَّهُ بَصِيرٌ بِالْعِبَادِ"3:20

In Qur'an, there are many verses indicating that Muhammad, peace be upon him, was sent by God to call all His servants (humans, jinn, Arabs, foreigners...) to worship Him. Thus, he obeyed God and so did.

· Another special characteristic is that the Messenger was the most perfect among the other prophets, peace be upon them. He was their leader, orator, imam and the last. All of them agreed that they will support and believe in him. God said: " And [recall, O People of the Scripture], when God took the covenant of the prophets, [saying], "Whatever I give you of the

Scripture and wisdom and then there comes to you a messenger confirming what is with you, you [must] believe in him and support him." [God] said, "Have you acknowledged and taken upon that My commitment?" They said, "We have acknowledged it." He said, "Then bear witness, and I am with you among the witnesses.", " وَإِذْ أَخَذَ اللَّهُ مِيثَاقَ النَّبِيِّينَ لَمَا آتَيْتُكُم مِّن كِتَابٍ وَحِكْمَةٍ ثُمَّ جَاءَكُمْ رَسُولٌ مُّصَدِّقٌ لِّمَا مَعَكُمْ لَتُؤْمِنُنَّ بِهِ وَلَتَنصُرُنَّهُ ۚ قَالَ أَأَقْرَرْتُمْ وَأَخَذْتُمْ عَلَىٰ ذَٰلِكُمْ إِصْرِي ۖ قَالُوا أَقْرَرْنَا ۚ قَالَ فَاشْهَدُوا وَأَنَا مَعَكُم مِّنَ الشَّاهِدِينَ" **3:81**. God meant that whatever scriptures or mercy sent to people, and then comes a Messenger sent by Him, they must back and believe in him. So, such matter is very peculiar to Muhammad, peace be upon him.

- He was born circumcised, as mentioned in the narration, but it is odd. It was also said that some other prophets were also born circumcised.

- Another matter that deems too specific is that miracle of each prophet ends by his death, yet Muhammad's is immortal. It is Qur'an, due to its inimitable wording and significance. God challenged humans and jinn to bring a similar book, but they failed, and this failure will continue till doomsday.

- The night journey to Jerusalem and midnight night journey to heaven is another peculiar feature. In this regard, Jibril said to Al-Buraq when it shied from Muhammad: "By your Lord! There is no one more honorable mounted you". Another narration said: " I tethered the animal to the ring used by the prophets". This implies that the same journey happened with the other prophets, but we know that such journey is an idiosyncratic feature to Muhammad. Hence, his rank in the Heaven is the highest and the nearest to the Throne. This is shown in the following narration: "Then beseech God to grant me Alwasilah, which is a high rank in the Heaven, fitting for only one of God's servants; and I hope that I will be that man."

· If Muhammad's nation agreed on a matter concerning the canons, their view is infallible, as such agreement shall become right and applicable, as set in books of fundamental concepts.

· He is the first whom the earth will be cleft open.

· On the doomsday, if people fall unconscious, he will be the first to gain consciousness. Abu Hurayrah said: a Jew said, "By Him Who gave superiority to Moses over all the people." A Muslim became furious at that and slapped the Jew in the face. The Jew went to the Messenger of God and informed him of what had happened between him and the Muslim. The Messenger of God said, "Don't give me superiority over Moses, for the people will fall unconscious on the doomsday and I will be the first to gain consciousness and behold! Moses will be there holding the side of God's Throne. I will not know whether Moses has been among those people who have become unconscious and then has regained consciousness before me or has been among those exempted by God from falling unconscious." Some attributed the meaning of this narration to the resurrection from death. Thus, the Messenger said: "Do not give a prophet superiority over another, for on the doomsday, all the people will fall unconscious and I will be the first to emerge from the earth and will see Moses standing and holding one of the legs of the Throne. I will not know whether Moses has fallen unconscious or the first unconsciousness was sufficient for him". Such context refers to gaining consciousness after losing it not after death.

· He is the owner of the great flag on the doomsday, he and his nation only will be resurrected on an elevated place of Earth. God will allow only them to prostrate. Ibn Magah said, on behalf of Gabara ibn Almughles Alhimany, Abu Almusawer, Abu Barda, Abu Mousa, quoting the Messenger: "When God gathers all creatures on the doomsday, permission will be given to the nation of Muhammad to prostrate, so they will prostrate to Him for a long time. Then it will be said: "Raise your heads, for a certain number of you will go to Hell-fire and these will be your ransom from Hell." This narration is unreliable, however, it meant that Muhammad's nation is the first to be judged on the doomsday.

· His place of revelation is the most honorable places. Ayad Alsabty said on behalf of Omar ibn Alkhatab that his grave is the most honorable place on Earth.

· He was not inherited after death, according to Abu Bakr and Abu Hurayrah, the Messenger said: "I should not be inherited, and whatever we leave, is to be spent in charity". Yet, Al-turmuzy quoted: "We, prophets, should not be inherited". According to this, such matter was common among all prophets, not only Muhammad.

What he had in common with the prophets was that they sleep with closing eyes, yet they were aware, during sleeping. In the narration mentioned by Sahih, the Messenger said: "Straighten your rows for I see you from behind my back". Abu Nasr ibn Alsabagh said: he was seeing what is before and behind him. In other words, it was a matter of sense. A narration by Abu Yaali Almously, "Prophets are alive in their graves praying"

Second Section

Features peculiar to the Messenger, among his nation, that may be common with other prophets

This will be mentioned according to jurisprudence sections Section of Faith

· He was infallible, in his deeds and words, as a fault was not approbated, so that it could not be his fault, so he was inspired to correct it. Many scholars viewed that he was not allowed to discretize, as he was given orders. Others said that he was allowed to discretize, but he had to avoid faults. Other opinion referred to that faults by him are not approbated. All opinions agreed that he was infallible, unlike the rest of his nation, yet if they all agreed on the same matter, it shall be applicable.

· Abu Alabbas ibn Alqas said that the Messenger was given of knowledge what is equal to the knowledge of all peoples. Albehqy cited the narration by ibn Omar, may God be pleased with him, on behalf of the Messenger: "While I was sleeping, I saw a bowl full of milk was brought to me and I drank of it (to my fill) till I noticed its wetness flowing (in my body). Then I gave the remaining of it to Omar." They asked, "O' Messenger of God! What have you interpreted (about the dream)? He said, " It is (Religious) knowledge."

· He was seeing the invisible to the others. In Sahih, according to Aisha, the Messenger said to Aisha: "Jibril sends greetings of Salam to you." She said: "And upon him be peace and the mercy of God and His blessings; you see what we do not.". In the narration of eclipse, he said: "By God, if you knew what I know, you would weep much and laugh little". Albehqy, on behalf of Alhakam, Mohamed ibn Ali ibn Duhaim, Ahmed ibn Hazem Alghafary, Obaidullah ibn Mousa, Ibrahim ibn Muhager, Mujahed, Moureq and Abu Zir, quoting the Messenger saying: "Has there [not] come upon man a period of time when he was not a thing [even] mentioned?" I see and hear what you do not, heaven has squeaked, and it has right to do so. By Him, in Whose Hand my soul is, there is not a space of four fingers in which there is not an angel who is prostrating his forehead before God, the Exalted. By God, if you knew what I know, you would laugh little, weep much, and you would not enjoy women in beds, but would go out to the open space beseeching God"

· God ordered the Messenger to prefer the afterworld to this world. He was prohibited to look forward to having the enjoyments of those who preferred the world.

· He was not taught the poetry. God said: "And We did not give Prophet Muhammad, knowledge of poetry, nor is it befitting for him", 36:69 "وَمَا عَلَّمْنَاهُ الشِّعْرَ وَمَا يَنْبَغِي لَهُ ۚ إِنْ هُوَ إِلَّا ذِكْرٌ وَقُرْآنٌ مُبِينٌ"

Abdullah ibn Omar said I heard the Messenger of God saying: "If I drink an antidote, or tie an amulet, or compose poetry, I am the type who does not care what he does. "Thus, it was said that he was prohibited to learn poetry.

· He was not able to write, God said: "Those who follow the Messenger, the unlettered prophet, whom they find written in what they have of the Torah and the Bible", " الَّذِينَ يَتَّبِعُونَ الرَّسُولَ النَّبِيَّ الْأُمِّيَّ الَّذِي يَجِدُونَهُ مَكْتُوبًا عِندَهُمْ فِي التَّوْرَاةِ وَالْإِنجِيلِ" 7:157

God also said: "And you did not recite before it any scripture, nor did you inscribe one with your right hand. Otherwise the falsifiers would have had [cause for] doubt.", " وَمَا كُنتَ تَتْلُو مِن قَبْلِهِ مِن كِتَابٍ وَلَا تَخُطُّهُ بِيَمِينِكَ ۖ إِذًا لَّارْتَابَ الْمُبْطِلُونَ" 29:48

Some claimed that he became literate before his death. This opinion is not proven, yet Albehqy quoted Abu Uqail Yehia ibn Almotawaqel, Migalid, Awen ibn Abdullah and his father saying: "Before his death, the Messenger, peace be upon him, was able to write and read. Some scholars claimed that the Messenger wrote treaty of Hudaybiyya, yet he denied this, clearly announcing that on pulpits. Such misunderstanding was raised from such tale: "The Messenger started to write: Muhammad ibn Abdullah, peace be upon him, agreed..." Yet, another tale was: "He ordered Ali to write, and he wrote: Muhammad ibn Abdullah, peace be upon him, agreed ..."

· Lying to him was not like lying to others. He was blessed by God blessings and peace. In this regard, a narration so supports: "whoever lies about me on purpose, then let him take his seat in the Fire." This narration is mentioned by eighty and some companions. It is mentioned in both Sahihs by Ali, Anas ibn Malik, Abu Hurayrah, Almughayra ibn Shaaba. It was mentioned by Albukhary, on behalf of Alzubair ibn Alawam, Salma ibn Alakwa, Abdullah ibn Amr; as following: "Convey (my teachings) to the people even if it was a single sentence and tell others the stories of Banu Israel (which have been taught to you), for it is not sinful to do so. And whoever tells a lie to me intentionally, will surely take his place in the (Hell) Fire."

All scholars agreed that whoever lies to Muhammad intentionally is wrongful. Some of them disagreed on the word "intentionally". Sheikh Abu Mohamed said that who intentionally did so, will go to Hell, many disagreed to his opinion. If he repented, shall he be reliable?

There are two opinions in this regard:

- Ahmed ibn Hanbal, Yehia ibn Main and Abu Bakr Alhumaidy said: no, as the Messenger said: "a lie to me is not like a lie to anyone else, whoever lies to me intentionally will take his seat in Hell". Some said that lying in general is a sin and so is lying to him. Whoever who repented and regretted lying to anyone else shall be forgiven and shall be reliable. Yet who lied to the Messenger shall not be reliable, out of differentiating between lying to the Messenger and lying to others.

- Most scholars said that who lied to the Messenger and repented shall be reliable, as who lied to the Messenger is equaled to a disbeliever, and who regretted disbelief, his repentance is accepted and shall be reliable. This opinion is true and the most common.

· Whoever sees the Messenger in dreams, is really seeing him, as mentioned in the narration: "Whoever saw me in a dream in fact saw me, for Satan does not appear in my form.", provided that he would be seen as in his life. It was agreed that whoever quoted him in dreams, such narration is not trustworthy, as dreams are from weak mind.

He did not misapprehend, out of backbiting. The following story so supports; on the day of conquest of Mecca, the Messenger, peace be upon him, shed the blood of Abdullah ibn Saad ibn Abu Sarh, when Othman ibn Afan, his foster-brother brought him, and made him stand before the Prophet and said: Accept the allegiance of the Messenger of God! He raised his head and looked at him three times, refusing him each time, but accepted his allegiance after the third time. Then turning to his companions, he said: Was not there a wise man among you who would stand up to him when he saw that I withheld my hand from accepting his allegiance, and kill him? They said: We did not know what you had in your heart, Messenger of God! Why did not you give us a signal with your eye? He said: "It is not advisable for a Prophet to play deceptive tricks with the eyes."

Section of Cleanness

·   He ordered people to perform ablution for each prayer, yet when this was somehow a burden, he ordered to use miswak (tooth cleanser). Abdullah ibn Hanzala ibn Abu Amer said that the Messenger, peace be upon him, ordered people to perform ablution for each prayer, whether its previous ablution is still valid or not, and when this was a burden, he ordered to use miswak instead. This shows that the miswak is a must. Imam Ahmed ibn Abbas so supported as he quoted the Messenger saying: "I was seriously ordered to use miswak, to the extent that I guessed that a verse or an inspiration would be revealed so concerning,"

Om Salma quoted the Messenger saying: "Jibril still recommends me to use miswak so much that I am worried about my teeth." Abdullah ibn Wahb, on behalf of Yehia ibn Abdullah ibn Salim, Amr Moula Almutlib, Almutlib ibn Abdullah and Aisha bint Abu Bakr, quoted the Messenger saying: "I keep using the miswak so much that I am afraid to lose my teeth." Imam Ahmed, on behalf of Wathela ibn Alasqaa, quoted the Messenger saying: "I was recommended to use the miswak so much that I was afraid that it would be an obligation." Hence, it was said that miswak is not a must but a plus.

·   The Messenger's ablution was not nullified by sleep. In this regard, ibn Abbas said that the Messenger slept till the calling for the prayer, so he prayed but did not perform ablution. Ibn Abbas based this on the narration by Aisha who asked the Messenger saying: "O' Messenger, do you go to bed before offering the Witr prayer?' He said, 'My eyes sleep, but my heart does not sleep.'" This narration was mentioned by Muslim and Albukhary. It was disagreed if the Messenger's ablution is nullified by touching women. Some supported the validity of the ablution, based on Aisha's narration, as she missed the Messenger who was in the mosque, so she went and touched him while he was saying: "I seek protection against Your Wrath in Your Pleasure. I seek protection in Your Pardon against Your chastisement, I am not capable of enumerating praising You as You have lauded Yourself".

Some said that the Messenger was being kissed and then prayed without ablution. The teller made this peculiar to him, but the opponents are not persuaded and see that such is not peculiar to the Messenger, unless an evidence existed.

Excerpts from The Prophetic Biography

☐ **Subject matter:**

Did the Messenger have wet dreams? Aisha in this regard said of the Messenger: "The Messenger would wake during Ramadan (fasting) in a state of major impurity without a wet dream, but on account of sexual intercourse and he would take a bath before dawn."

Explanation in this point should be offered, as it was said if ejaculation is surplus, so it is not a problem. If it is an act of devil, the Messenger is not questioned, as it may be of syncope. In a narration by Aisha, it was said that the Messenger bathed after syncope more than once.

· Abu Abbas ibn Alqas said that the Messenger was not forbidden to stay in the mosque on major impurity. This was supported by narration of Alturmuzy, on behalf of Salim ibn Abu Hafsa, Atia and Abu Said, who quoted the Messenger saying: "O' Ali, it is not permissible for anyone to be Junub (on major impurity) in this mosque except for you and I". Alturmuzy said that this narration is fine but odd as we only knew it from this source. Many scholars view this narration is unreliable. Yet, Dhirar ibn Surd refers it to transit permission, but it is still problematic, as transit permission is awarded to all people, so it is not specifically granted to someone. However, such transit permission is not allowed in Alnabawi mosque for anyone except Muhammad, peace be upon him and Ali, thus he said: "O' Ali, it is not permissible for anyone to be Junub (on major impurity) in this mosque except for you and I".

Madhoug Alzouhly, on behalf of Gasra bint Dagaga and Om Salma, quoted the Messenger saying when he once a day entered the mosque yard: "The mosque is not permissible for anyone sexually impure or any menstruating woman, except the Messenger, Ali ibn Abu Talib, Fatima, Alhassan and Alhussein, I named them, so that it can be clear enough". Albukhary said that this narration in doubtable. So, it was said that this was not the Messenger's attitude.

· The Messenger was known for his hair's cleanness, as shown in the narration by Imam Muslim, according to Anas, as the Messenger when shaved his hair for pilgrimage, he ordered Abu Talha to distribute it over the people. This could be a specific feature if we confirmed that shaved hair of anyone else alive is impure. Ibn Oudai said, on behalf of ibn Abu Fudik, Burih ibn Omar ibn Safina, his father and his grandfather: the Messenger underwent cupping and ordered ibn Abu Fudik to take that blood and bury it far from animals and birds. Ibn Abu Fudik drank it, who was asked by the Messenger about the blood and admitted that he drank it, so the Messenger laughed. This narration is inaccurate. Albehqy quoted Abu Alhassan ibn Abdan, Ahmed ibn Obaid, Mohammed ibn Ghalib, Mousa ibn Ishmael, Obaid ibn Alqasim, Amir ibn Abdullah ibn Alzubair and his father; that the Messenger when performed cupping asked Abdullah ibn Alzubair to hide his blood away from dogs and people, but he drank it. When he was asked by the Messenger, he lied. Such narration is not reliable and nullified by Yehia ibn Moen.

Thus some pointed to the purity of his wastes, referring to what mentioned by Albehqy ibn Abu Nasr ibn Qatada, Abu Alhassan Mohamed ibn Ahmed Alattar, Ahmed ibn Alhassan ibn Abd Aljabar, Yehia ibn Moen, Hagag and ibn Garih who said: Hakima bint Omaima, on behalf of her mother said that the Messenger was urinating in a goblet of rods then put the same under his bed. He wanted the goblet, but found it empty, he said to Barka, a servant of Om Habiba: "where is the urine?" she said: I drank it. But it is not reliable.

Section of Prayer

Imam Ahmed and Albehqy, on behalf of Akrama and Ibn Abbas, quoted the Messenger, peace be upon him saying: "there are things I do as obligations, yet for you they are optional: The Sacrifice, Witr Prayer and Forenoon Prayer". According to this narration, these three are turned to musts. Sheikh Taqeyeldin ibn Alsalah said that the scholars were not sure if miswak was a must for him. They confirmed that he was obliged to perform Forenoon Prayer, the Sacrifice and Witr Prayer, they so supported by the narration above which is deemed unreliable. If they were unsure about the three things mentioned therein and were sure about the miswak, this would be more persuading.

Regarding the three above matters, Sheikh Abu Zakaria Al-nawawy talked about the uncertainty of some scholars about the same, yet some of them went with the desirability thereof by the Messenger.

Such opinion is more likely because:

- It is based on the above narration, despite its unreliability.

- It is proven in both Sahihs that Witr Prayer was performed by the Messenger on the camel, so it is not an obligation, as if it was so, he would not perform it on the camel.

- For the Forenoon Prayer, Aisha said that he only performed it when he returned after a journey. Therefore, if it is obligatory for him, he would preserve it. He was also quoted saying that he was performing it in two prostrations.

□ **Subject matter:**

For the voluntary late-night prayer which is Witr Prayer, Imam Ahmed on behalf of ibn Omar quoted the Messenger saying: "Witr prayer is performed as one prostration at the late night".

Most scholars said this prayer was obligatory for him, according to God's words: "And from [part of] the night, pray with it as additional [worship] for you; it is expected that your Lord will resurrect you to a praised rank." " وَمِنَ اللَّيْلِ فَتَهَجَّدْ بِهِ نَافِلَةً لَّكَ

"عَسَىٰ أَن يَبْعَثَكَ رَبُّكَ مَقَامًا مَّحْمُودًا 17:79. Atia ibn Said Aloufy referred that "additional worship for you" means that it is special for the Messenger.

Orwa, on behalf of Aisha said that the Messenger used to offer late-night prayers till his feet became swollen. Aisha wondered saying: "God has forgiven you, your faults of the past and those to follow." On that, he said, "Shouldn't I be a thankful slave of God?"

Albehqy quoted, on behalf of Mousa ibn Abdulrahman Alsananey, Hisham ibn Orwa, his father and Aisha, the Messenger saying: "Three things are obligatory to me, and optional to you; Witr Prayer, Miswak, late-night prayer". This narration is not reliable.

Sheikh Abu Hamid, on behalf of Imam Abu Abdullah Alsahfie, said: late-night prayer was set as an obligation for the Messenger and his nation. It was a must in the beginning of Islam. Sheikh Abu Amr ibn Alsalah said: this is true, according to all narrations, such as narration of Saad ibn Hisham, on behalf of Aisha. Abu Zakaria Alnawawy also so confirmed.

Hisham ibn Saad once visited Aisha. He said: "O Mother of the Believers, tell me about the late-night prayer of the Messenger." She said: "Don't you read Al-Muzzamil?" I said: "Yes." She said: "God instructed about such prayer at the beginning of this Surah. So, the Messenger of God and his companions performed late-night prayer for one year. God withheld the latter part of this surah for twelve months, then he revealed the lessening (of this duty) at the end of this surah, so this prayer became voluntary after it had been obligatory. God said: "And from [part of] the night, pray with it as additional [worship] for you." "وَمِنَ اللَّيْلِ فَتَهَجَّدْ بِهِ نَافِلَةً لَّكَ" 17:79. This means that late-night prayer is an optional worship.

☐ **Subject matter:**

He missed post-noon prostrations, so he performed them after the Afternoon Prayer. He kept performing such prayer. Such prostrations were peculiar to him according to some scholars. Others refer that they were for others.

☐ **Subject matter:**

He was performing his additional prayers sitting as when standing, unless he was excused, unlike others, whose prayers in the same case are considered half. Muslim, on behalf of Abdullah ibn Amr, quoted the Messenger saying: "Performing prayer while sitting is a half prayer. Then I visited him and saw him praying in seat, so I put my hand on his, he said: what is up with Abdullah ibn Amr? I said: O' Messenger, you said that performing prayer while sitting is a half prayer and you now are doing so. He replied: yes, but I am not like you.

☐ **Subject matter**:

Who was going to perform prayer, if called by the Messenger, he should obey, according to narration of Abu Said ibn Almoely in Albukhary's Sahih. Yet, Alouzaei said, on behalf of Sheikh Makehoul ibn Abu Muslim Shehrab, that the mother must also be obeyed even at prayers. According to Garig Alrahib, his mother called him while he was getting ready for prayer, yet he ignored her for the prayer, and he so repeated triply. Thus, she asked God to take revenge from him and God responded. Such tale was narrated repeatedly. Yet most scholars view that it is not allowed to talk to people during prayer. Only an exception according to Imam Ahmed, is to talk to the prayer leader, notifying him of what he may neglect in the prayer.

☐ **Subject matter:**

The Messenger did not perform the funeral prayer for whoever died with an unsettled debt. Albukhary mentioned such narration, on behalf of Salma ibn Alakwaa. Yet the scholars controverted about if it was prohibited or abhorred. The Messenger said: "If a Muslim dies leaving some property, the property will go to his heirs; and if he leaves a debt, we will handle it." Some said the Messenger used to settle the debt out of duty, others said out of generosity.

· If the Messenger, peace be upon him, prayed for the dead, God would fill their graves with light and good, according to a narration mentioned in Muslim's Sahih, on behalf of Aisha.

The Messenger once passed by two graves, said: "They are being punished, but they are not being punished for anything major. One of them was heedless about preventing urine from getting on his clothes, and the other used to walk about spreading malicious gossip." Then he grabbed a fresh twig and split it into two parts, to plan them on each grave and then said: "Ask God to mitigate their punishment as long as these twigs remain fresh.", Ibn Abbas so mentioned.

☐ **Subject Matter**

The Messenger was too sick, Abdulla ibn Masoud said to him: O' Messenger, you are too sick. The Messenger said: yes, my sickness is equal to that of two men. Abdullah said: because you are awarded twice? He replied: yes.

☐ Subject Matter

He did not die, till God has offered him to choose from much world-life or Heaven. He preferred Heaven to the world-life. It is proven in both Sahihs, according to Aisha's narration.

☐ **Subject Matter**

God also barred the earth to get corpses of the prophets decayed. This is proven by Shadad ibn Aws's narration.

Section of Zakat

☐ **Subject matter:**

He was prohibited to take money of Zakat, either obligatory or voluntary; he said: " It is not lawful for Muhammad or the family of Muhammad". Muslim, on behalf of Abu Hurayrah stated that the Messenger was eating what he was offered as a gift but not as alms. After his death, people misinterpreted and stopped paying Zakat and did not pay it to Abu Bakr, but he insisted till they realized their obligations and paid Zakat.

Section of Fasting

Uninterrupted fasting was allowed to the Messenger, thus he barred his nation from uninterrupted fasting. Some of the companions said: You yourself fast uninterruptedly, whereupon he said: I am not like you. I am fed and supplieddrink (by God).

It was controverted if the Messenger meant by "fed and supplied (by God)", literally (physically) or spiritually. Yet, it is logical to be spiritually so that the uninterrupted fasting could be achieved.

☐ **Subject matter:**

Some said that if he began a voluntary fasting, he would complete it. Yet this is not reliable, and it is refuted by Aisha'a narration: "Then he came to us and I said to him: someone has offered us some Hais as a gift (it is a type of cakes). He then said: Show it to me. I had been fasting since this morning, and he ate from it."

Section of pilgrimage

· It was said that if he attracted by something, he must say: "There is no life worth living except the life of the Hereafter". This is based on the narration mentioned by Albukhary, on behalf of Sahl ibn Saad, quoting the Messenger saying on the day of the battle of the Trench, when he started to dig the trench while we were leaving: "So forgive the Immigrants and the Ansar".

Alshafei said on behalf of Said, ibn Garig, Humaid Alaarag, Mujahed, quoting the Messenger: "I am at Your service, O God, I am at Your service. You have no partner. I am at Your service. Praise and blessing belong to You, and the Kingdom. You have no partner" He was saying that frequently.

We view that this narration does not refer to any obligation, it was just a matter of desirability.

☐ **Subject matter:**

He was allowed to enter Mecca for only one day, so he so entered not for pilgrimage, when about twenty Meccans were killed. So, did Islam spread in Mecca by war or peace? Alshafei said it was the victory by peace. The Messenger in his sermon on that morning, said "If anyone seeks a concession on the basis of fighting with the Messenger, tell him that God permitted His Messenger, but not you".

Section of food

He was forbidden to intake onion, garlic and leek. This is supported by the Messenger's narration; "Once a plate full of cooked vegetables was brought to the Messenger. Detecting a bad smell from it, he asked about the dish and was informed of the kinds of vegetables it contained. He then said, "Bring it near," and so it was brought near to one of his companions who was with him. When the Messenger saw it, he disliked eating it and said (to his companion), "Eat, for I talk in secret to ones whom you do not talk to." It was somehow problematic. It was not prohibited, just abhorred. As an evidence, a narration by Imam Muslim, on behalf of Abu Ayoub is as following: "a garlic-containing food was brought to the Messenger, but he so refused. Abu Ayoub asked: Is it prohibited? The Messenger said: no, I just dislike it. Abu Ayoub said: I dislike what you dislike.

In the same regard, and concerning the dabb-lizard, the Messenger, peace be upon him said: "I neither eat it nor make it a taboo, yet I disgust eating it. Khalid ibn Alwalid said: is it a taboo, O' Messenger? He said: "No, but it is not found in the land of my people and that is why I do not like eating it". The Messenger also said, "Leave it, for destruction comes from being near disease." Physicians also forbade eating such animal, as it causes bad mood.

□ **Subject matter:**

Albukhary, on behalf of Abu Guhifa said quoting the Messenger: "I do not take my meals while leaning (against something)." It was said that he was forbidden to do that. Alnawawy said it is not prohibited but abhorred. So, it is not peculiar to him, as the Messenger also abhorred for others to eat while leaning, even it is interpreted either as recumbency, for the harm it brought about, just as drinking while standing, or being cross-legged, according to Alkhataby and other linguists. The latter interpretation seems more logical, as being cross-legged refers to the pompous and despotic character.

□ **Subject matter:**

Abu Alabbas ibn Alqas said that the Messenger, peace be upon him, was prohibited to eat from food he was not invited to. He was quoted saying: "Who does not accept an invitation which he receives has disobeyed God and His Messenger, and he who enters without invitation enters as a thief and goes out as a raider."

□ **Subject matter:**

It was said that if anybody asked the Messenger for a food which is the last at his house, he must give it to him, out of charity and generosity. In this regard, God said: "The Prophet is worthier of the believers than themselves", " النَّبِيُّ أَوْلَىٰ بِالْمُؤْمِنِينَ مِنْ أَنفُسِهِمْ" 33:6

This narration is corresponding to the previous verse: "None of you is a believer till I am dearer to him than his child, his father and the whole of mankind."

☐ **Subject matter:**

Albukhary said, on behalf of Alsaab ibn Gathama: "There is no (permission for) protected land except for God and His Prophet". Some said that such matter is peculiar to him. Others said it is allowed to others, for an advantage, as Alnaqie which is protected by the Messenger and Alsirf and Alrabza which are protected by Omar ibn Alkhatab.

Gifts

☐ **Subject matter:**

The Messenger, peace be upon him, was accepting gifts. This was mentioned in the Sahih of Albukhary, according to Aisha, may God be pleased with her. Such gifts were for making peace. For gifts given for workers, they are booty theft, as they are considered bribes.

☐ **Subject matter:**

Concerning this verse, "And whatever you give for interest to increase within the wealth of people will not increase with God", 30:39 "وَمَا آتَيْتُم مِّن رِّبًا لِّيَرْبُوَ فِي أَمْوَالِ النَّاسِ فَلَا يَرْبُو عِندَ اللَّهِ", Zakaria ibn Oudai, on behalf of ibn Almubarak, Alouzaie, ibn Ataa said it is the lawful usury to offer a gift for a bigger one, it is not a sin. Yet the Messenger was prohibited from such act, according to this verse: "And do not confer favor to acquire more", " وَلَا تَمْنُن تَسْتَكْثِرُ" 74:6

Religious duties

☐ **Subject matter:**

The Messenger, peace be upon him, was not inherited, but properties left by him is for charity, as mentioned in both Sahihs, as Abu Bakr said that Fatima asked him about her share from her father's inheritance, he told her: I heard the Messenger saying: "our property should not be inherited, and whatever we leave, is to be spent in charity". And according to Abu Hurayrah, the Messenger said: "My heirs must not distribute a dinar, from my assets, after deducting the expenditure of my women (family), and the workers. whatever is left over must be spent in charity"

Section of marriage

It includes the features peculiar to the Prophet, peace be upon him. It will be mentioned according to the scholars.

Part 1
Obligations to him solely

☐ **Subject matter:**

The Messenger was ordered by God to let his wives choose from the temporary beauty of the world-life or the lasting beauty of the afterlife. He said: "O Prophet, say to your wives, "If you should desire the worldly life and its adornment, then come, I will provide for you and give you a gracious release. But if you should desire God and His Messenger and the home of the Hereafter - then indeed, God has prepared for the doers of good among you a great reward.", " يَا أَيُّهَا النَّبِيُّ قُل لِّأَزْوَاجِكَ إِن كُنتُنَّ تُرِدْنَ الْحَيَاةَ الدُّنْيَا وَزِينَتَهَا فَتَعَالَيْنَ أُمَتِّعْكُنَّ وَأُسَرِّحْكُنَّ سَرَاحًا جَمِيلًا، وَإِن كُنتُنَّ تُرِدْنَ اللَّهَ وَرَسُولَهُ وَالدَّارَ الْآخِرَةَ فَإِنَّ اللَّهَ أَعَدَّ لِلْمُحْسِنَاتِ مِنكُنَّ أَجْرًا عَظِيمًا" 33:28-29

It was controverted if was a must or a desirability. Alnawawy and others referred to the must.

It was also controverted if the answers of the Messenger's wives were required immediately or later. Ibn Alsabagh said that it was not required immediately, based on the Messenger's narration talking to Aisha: "You do not have to hasten (in making a decision) until you have consulted your parents"

Part two
Marriage issues he was solely prohibited from

☐ **Subject matter:**

He was forbidden from refusing to release a woman willing to divorce, unlike others who should hold on staying with their wives.

☐ **Subject matter:**

Was the Messenger allowed to marry the non-muslim? One view supported that he was not allowed to do so, based on the narration of the Messenger, as he said: "My wives in the worldly life are the same in the afterlife." Another view argued that it was allowed, as his non-muslim women converted to Islam. Actually, such narration is not reliable, as it was only said by some companions.

Concerning his concubinage of the non-muslim bondwomen and his marriage to the muslim ones, there are several views. The most accurate is that the Messenger, peace be upon him, was allowed to concubine the non-muslim and was not allowed to marry the muslim bondwoman.

The most scholars deduced that the Messenger was not allowed to marry the non-muslim bondwoman.

Part three

Marriage issues he was solely allowed

☐ **Subject matter:**

The Messenger, peace be upon him, died, on having nine women.

☐ **Subject matter:**

His marriage contraction was becoming valid, upon endowment, according to God's words: "A believing woman if she gives herself to the Prophet [and] if the Prophet wishes to marry her, [this is] only for you, excluding the [other] believers", "وَامْرَأَةً مُّؤْمِنَةً إِن وَهَبَتْ نَفْسَهَا لِلنَّبِيِّ إِنْ أَرَادَ النَّبِيُّ أَن يَسْتَنكِحَهَا خَالِصَةً لَّكَ مِن دُونِ الْمُؤْمِنِينَ" 33:50

Was he limited by the irrevocable divorce (represented in divorcing three time)? It was said yes, he was abiding by the same. Others said no, he was not limited as he was not limited in four wives.

☐ **Subject matter:**

He was allowed to marry without a proxy for the wife or witnesses, as Zainab bint Gahsh was boasting as she got married to the Messenger with no proxy but God, unlike the other wives who got married to him under proxy of their families.

☐ **Subject matter:**

Was he allowed to have intercourse while being on pilgrimage?

One view referred that he was not allowed, based on the narration mentioned by Muslim, on behalf of Othman, that the Messenger said: "A Muhrim (one in the state of Ihram) must neither marry himself, nor arrange the marriage of another one, nor should he make the proposal of marriage." Others argued that it is was permissible to him, as ibn Abbas said that the Messenger, peace be upon him, married to Maymouna while on pilgrimage. Yet this opinion was refuted by what was mentioned by Muslim, according to Maymouna herself that he had intercourse with her after finishing his pilgrimage.

☐ **Subject matter:**

Was he obliged to stay with his wives each equally? The narrations state that he actually was obliged to do so, as when he got sick, he was visiting them all, and eventually he asked them to be nursed at Aisha's, and they accepted. On the contrary, Abu Said Alastakhry viewed that he was not obliged to do so, as God said: "You, [O Muhammad], may put aside whom you will of them or take to yourself whom you will", " تُرْجِي مَن تَشَاءُ مِنْهُنَّ

وَتُؤْوِي إِلَيْكَ مَن تَشَاءُ"33:51

☐ **Subject matter:**

His release to Safeya was as a dowry for her. Some assumed that release was in return for the marriage, so she surrendered to marriage for her freedom. Yet, such opinion was refuted as manumission can be a dowry.

Part four
Virtues peculiar to him

His wives were mothers of believers, as God said: "The Prophet is worthier of the believers than themselves, and his wives are [in the position of] their mothers", " النَّبِيُّ أَوْلَىٰ بِالْمُؤْمِنِينَ

33:6."مِنْ أَنفُسِهِمْ ۖ وَأَزْوَاجُهُ أُمَّهَاتُهُمْ" This motherhood refers to respect, obedience, ingratitude barring and aggrandizement.

Was the Messenger called father of believers? Some goes with affirmation, supported by "The Prophet is worthier of the believers than themselves, and his wives are [in the position of] their mothers",**33:6** " النَّبِيُّ أَوْلَىٰ بِالْمُؤْمِنِينَ مِنْ أَنفُسِهِمْ ۖ وَأَزْوَاجُهُ أُمَّهَاتُهُمْ". Others negate that supported by such verse "Muhammad is not the father of [any] one of your men", " مَّا كَانَ مُحَمَّدٌ أَبَا أَحَدٍ مِّن رِّجَالِكُمْ"**33:40**

□ **Subject matter:**

His wives are the best nation's women, as they were rewarded twice, unlike others. Of them Khadija and Aisha were the best.

□ **Subject matter:**

His wives are prohibited to marry after his death, as they are his wives in the Heaven. If a widow does not marry after her husband's death, she will be his afterlife wife. Abu Aldardaa's wife on his death, told him: you previously asked my family to marry me and they accepted, today I am marrying you myself. So, he said: do not marry after me. Since, after his death, Moawia proposed to her, but she refused. Albehqy mentioned on behalf of Eisa ibn Abdulrahman Alsulmi, ibn Isaac quoting Huthaifa saying to her wife: "if you are happy being my wife in the Heaven, do not marry after me. Women will go to their last husband in the Heaven. Thus, the Prophet's wives were prohibited to marry after him as they are his afterlife wives.

It was controverted about these women he divorced. Some go with that these divorced women who had intercourse with him are not allowed to marry others. Alshafei supported the absolute prohibition. Abu Hurayrah also supported the same, based on God's words: "his wives are [in the position of] their mothers", 33:6"وَأَزْوَاجُهُ أُمَّهَاتُهُمْ"

Concerning the bondwomen he left by his death, some scholars said that they were allowed to marry others after death. This opinion is supported by the verse of freedom of the choice, that if she was allowed to choose another man, she should not be offered the freedom of choice.

☐ Subject matter:

Whoever insulted the Messenger, peace be upon him, should be killed, either a man or a woman. According to a narration by ibn Abbas, a blind man killed his son's mother as she defamed the Messenger. In this regard, the Messenger said: "Oh people! Be witnesses that no blood money is to be paid for her". A man insulted Abu Bakr but he was not killed as such permission was peculiar to the Messenger. Ibrahim ibn Saad, on behalf of Al-zahry, Abu Salma and Abu Hurayrah, said: nobody is killed for insulating anyone but the Prophet.

☐ Subject matter:

If the Messenger, peace be upon him, defamed someone, such defaming shall be deemed an atonement. Abu Hurayrah quoted the Messenger, peace be upon him, saying: "I have held covenant with You, God which You would not break, so for any believer whom I curse or beat, make that an expiation for him on the doomsday"

Concerning Jihad (seeking God's path)

☐   Subject matter:

If he got armored to be ready for a war, he was not allowed to take off his armor until God so permitted. On the day of battle of Uhud, the Messenger went to be armored. Some of the troops said; "O' Messenger, if you want to stay in Medina, so do." He replied: "if a prophet gets armored, he shall not stay far from the battle". The scholars said that this was a duty, he was not allowed to take off his armor but after battling.

☐   Subject matter:

The Messenger, peace be upon him, was obliged to consult his companions concerning war. God said: "consult them in the matter" "3:159"وَشَاوِرْهُمْ فِي الْأَمْرِ"

Abu Hurayrah said no one was more consulting with his companions than the Messenger. The Messenger was not in need to consult others, but he wanted the future rulers to follow his example. Thus, if this is the case, such could not be a peculiar feature.

☐   Subject matter:

He was obliged to be patient battling the enemy, even if its troops are more than his. In a narration, the Messenger said to Orwa, referring to Quraish: "I will fight with them defending my Cause till I get killed".

☐   Subject matter:

We previously quoted the Messenger saying: "It is not advisable for a Prophet to play deceptive tricks with the eyes." However, it was said that he was allowed to play tricks in wars, as he said: "War is a game". He already did so at the battle of Trench, when he ordered Nuaim to backbite Quraish and Qurayza, so he managed to get them breakup. Instead, enmity was implanted between both parties.

☐   Subject matter:

He was allowed to pick what he wanted from the booty, a slave, bondwoman, weapon; before being distributed over the Muslims. This was mentioned and proven in the narrations. He was also entitled to take the fifth of the fifth of any booty as well as four-fifths of the loots.

His judgments

He was allowed to issue judgments, according to his knowledge. This is supported by Hind bint Otba, when she complained her husband's miserliness to the Messenger. He said: "Take from his property what is customary which may suffice you and your children". The narration is mentioned in both Sahihs, by Aisha, may God be pleased with her.

He was allowed to issue judgements for himself and his children and witness for himself and his children. Other prosecution witnesses were accepted.

☐ Subject matter:

It was said that whoever disdain the Messenger, peace be upon him, shall be a disbeliever.

☐ Subject matter:

Others may be named Muhammad, as a good omen. However, concerning taking the epithet of "Abu Alqasem – father of Qasem", the scholars have three views:

One of them refers to the absolute prohibition, according to Alshafei, Albehqy, Abdullah ibn Muhammad Albaghwy and Abu Alqasem ibn Asaker Adimashky, as they quoted the Messenger, peace be upon him, saying: "Name yourselves after me, but do not call yourselves by my Kuniya (Abu Alqasem).

Another view refers to the absolute permission. Such view was adopted by Alnawawy, as prohibition was only applied during the Messenger's life.

A third view refers that it is allowed to those whose name is not Muhammad, so that the Messenger's name and epithet. Such view was also adopted by Abu Alqasem Abdulkarim Alrifaei.

☐ Subject matter:

It was mentioned that his decedents from his daughters should be attributed to him. Albukhary, on behalf of Abu Bakra, said that the Messenger of God said about Alhasan ibn Ali. "This son of mine is a leader, and I hope God may reconcile two parties of my community by means of him."

☐ Subject matter:

Relatives and acquaintances shall not benefit anybody on the doomsday, but this is not applicable to his relatives and acquaintances. God said: "So when the Horn is blown, no relationship will there be among them that Day, nor will they ask about one another.", " فَإِذَا نُفِخَ فِي الصُّورِ فَلَا أَنسَابَ بَيْنَهُمْ يَوْمَئِذٍ وَلَا يَتَسَاءَلُونَ"22:101 .

In the same regard, Abu Said Mouli ibn Hashim, on behalf of Abdullah ibn Gaefer, Om Bakr bint Almosawer ibn Makhrama, Abdullah ibn Abu Rafie, quoted the Messenger saying: "Indeed Fatima is a part of me, I am harmed by what harms her and I am pleased by what makes her pleased." When Omar ibn Alkhatab, may God be pleased with him proposed to Om Kalthoum bint Ali ibn Abu Talib, he refused as she was young, Omar said: I heard the Messenger saying: "Relatives and acquaintances will not benefit on the doomsday, but mine", so I like to get related to the Messenger, so Ali agreed to get her married to Omar.

The scholars cleared that this means that his nation will attribute to him on the doomsday, and nations of the other prophets will not be attributed to them. Others said that this means attributing to the Messenger only will benefit the attributers. Such opinion is more reasonable. In the same concern, God said: "And [mention] the Day when We will resurrect among every nation a witness over them from themselves.", " وَيَوْمَ نَبْعَثُ فِي كُلِّ أُمَّةٍ شَهِيدًا عَلَيْهِم مِّنْ أَنفُسِهِم". 16:89

He also said: "And for every nation is a messenger. So, when their messenger comes, it will be judged between them in justice, and they will not be wronged", " وَلِكُلِّ أُمَّةٍ رَّسُولٌ ۖ فَإِذَا جَاءَ رَسُولُهُمْ قُضِيَ بَيْنَهُم بِالْقِسْطِ وَهُمْ لَا يُظْلَمُونَ" 10:47

There are several verses referring to that each nation is called by its messenger.

ABOUT THE AUTHOR

Ismail ibn Kathir was a highly influential historian, exegete and scholar during the Mamluk era in Syria. An expert on tafsir and faqīh, he wrote several books, including a fourteen-volume universal history.